TEENY WEENIES

AND OTHER SHORT SUBJECTS

MATT KAILEY

outskirtspress
DENVER, COLORADO

For you

Contents

Introduction

AS I WRITE this, it's been fourteen years since I sat in a barbershop chair and watched my shoulder-length, TV-anchor-woman hair fall to the floor around me in a reddish-brown cascade. It's been fourteen years since I dumped two overflowing makeup bags into the trash and donated at least twenty bottles of nail polish, along with a complete (and rather stylish) woman's wardrobe, to the Gender Identity Center of Colorado. And it's been fourteen years since I made the decision not to quietly transition and attempt to assimilate into mainstream society, where I was truly at home as a straight woman, but to write, speak, and be otherwise loudmouthed about transgender issues in general, and specifically about my own. Fourteen years ago, in 1997, I found my voice.

The first legitimate thing I ever wrote was a short story in seventh grade. It got rave reviews from the teacher, who instructed me to read it out loud to the class. The story was about a boy who wanted a horse for his birthday, but got a bicycle instead. It could just as easily have been about a girl in the same situation – but it wasn't.

My next serious attempt at writing was when I was seventeen, and I wrote a "novel" about a seventeen-year-old boy who fell in love with an older woman. She eventually left him, but not before they both got involved with drugs and she got pregnant and had an abortion behind his back. I thought it was worthy of a Pulitzer. I showed it to my parents, who responded, "Are you trying to tell us something?" Yes, but I didn't know what it was that I was trying to tell them (and the Pulitzer people never called).

Later, in my college creative writing class, my instructor said, "Your stories are really good, but you need to write some with female main characters. You can't always write from a male point of view. You're a woman, after all." I didn't disagree. Instead, I tried my hand at stories with female leads. My stories were no longer "really good." In fact, my stories were no longer – I just quit writing.

Fourteen years ago, I started writing again, and haven't stopped since. I might not have gained the singing voice that I had hoped testosterone would give me (all of the other guys were worried about losing theirs, so I figured I had a good chance of getting one – wrong again). Without my makeup and big hair, I'm definitely no longer the hottest one in the room (but that would have run its course no matter what – time marches on). But I can finally write, with no one telling me that I have to "write like a girl" (they still tell me that I run like a girl – I tell them I've had a lot of practice).

Teeny Weenies and Other Short Subjects is a collection of essays (with one short story thrown in for good measure) that I have written over the past few years. A couple have been published elsewhere. Most have never been anywhere other than on my computer, so it's time I took them out for a spin.

These essays cover different places and spaces in my life, and they by no means create a comprehensive picture. When *Just Add Hormones: An Insider's Guide to the Transsexual Experience* was released in 2005, some readers complained that I told them nothing about my childhood – they had no idea how I came to be who I am. All I can say is that if I ever figure that out, I'll let you know. But the first essays presented in this collection might offer some explanation – or excuse.

The essays in the first section, "A Short Childhood," are best read in order, as they are presented chronologically, from childhood through early adolescence. The rest deal with various stages, ages, and experiences. Together, they make up bits and pieces of a life that is at the same time seemingly endless and very short – like my teeny weenie.

(Note: A (slightly more erotic) version of the short story "Teeny Weenies, Inc." was originally published in *Best Transgender Erotica* (Circlet Press, 2002), edited by Hanne Blank and Raven Kaldera. A version of the essay "Most Changed Since High School" was originally published in *5280* magazine (June, 2006).)

A Short Childhood

YOU WON'T FIND my childhood in any psychology text-books about transsexuality. All my "gender stuff" was pretty hit and miss, and it's no wonder. In the 1950s and '60s, in the Midwestern United States, in a two-heterosexual-parent, white, semi-middle-class family, there was no such thing as gender fluidity. There was no such thing as gender diversity. There was no such thing as questioning. And there was definitely no such thing as the Internet. We did, however, have television. We had magazines. We had a world of influences with little information.

I knew I was a girl, and I never questioned that fact. I later came to question why such an accident occurred, but I never doubted the reality of it. I spent the first few years of my life internalizing what it meant to be a girl (or what I thought it meant), the next few years doubting it all, and the years after that – in adolescence and adulthood – revisiting what I had originally "learned" and trying to figure out a way to recapture it. After all, I *was* a girl – and even though things went astray for a while, I eventually figured out what I had to do … before I really figured out what I *had* to do.

There She Is

WHEN I WAS growing up, the Miss America Pageant was greeted with a reverence usually reserved for Christmas. The whole neighborhood shut down, and everyone drew their curtains and gathered around the television set as if it were a decorated tree. The phone didn't ring and no neighbor dared to come calling. There was serious business going on inside those houses, and it had to do with the armchair judging of the most important race in the country. Fewer people probably watched the election returns than the crowning of the most beautiful woman in America.

There was no doubting the importance of this contest. At five years old, I literally believed that a group of judges visited every one of the fifty states, lined up all the women of a certain age against a plain white wall, and chose the most alluring of the bunch to come to Atlantic City for the contest. It was the ultimate goal in life – to be publicly recognized for the most important accomplishment known to womanhood, and to get a crown, a brand new car, and a scholarship besides. There was simply no better deal in existence.

The Miss America Pageant, while not nearly as time-intensive as the whole rigmarole surrounding Christmas, could still take up the better part of a week. There was the endless talking about it at school, the new Big Chief tablets that had to be purchased to keep track of each contestant, preparations for the Barbie-doll beauty pageant that took place in my bedroom after the real contest, and the food that had to be prepared for the big night. My mother favored popcorn with real melted butter, Coca-Cola in cartoon jelly glasses, and a bowl of Hershey's Kisses. Across the street at my friend Sandy's house, I knew they would be having salami, cheese, crackers, and tomato juice. The ritual was the same – only the trappings differed based on local custom.

I was never conflicted over the questionable wisdom of pairing greasy and fattening snacks with the voyeuristic ritual of watching thin women parading around in swimming suits and high heels. It was just a part of what made the night special. And watching my mother chow down on the junk, I never believed that it could be dangerous. She was as beautiful as any of the contestants, and she even had her own title – Posture Queen, which she'd been granted in finishing school in a contest that I was certain was only a prelude to the real thing, especially since she even got a sash.

She could easily have been Miss America if my father hadn't interfered by proposing – she was a majorette in high school, so could have aced the talent competition with her baton-twirling routine. It must have been a tough choice, but she opted for the family security and the used car and still remained slender and beautiful, even with her extensive popcorn habit.

It was my mother who first made me realize not only the individual importance of being beautiful, but the actual responsibility that a woman had to herself and her family to either naturally possess this attribute or learn how to create it. My mother naturally possessed it, which then gave her the duty to enhance it – nobody got a free lunch. And although there weren't nearly as many cosmetic aids then as there are now, the Avon lady and the local Rexall drugstore offered enough of a selection that no woman had an excuse not to look her radiant best.

My mother stockpiled Avon products in much the same way that our next-door neighbors gathered Hershey bars and batteries during the Cuban missile crisis, but Avon was much more of a necessity. If the Russians really did bomb us, our neighbors might be able to listen to their transistor radio and run their flashlight, but how good would they really look doing it? I was pretty sure that, once the mushroom cloud cleared, the cache in my mother's bathroom would be far more valuable than a brown paper bag full of candy bars in some underground bunker.

When we first moved into our new house in Cheyenne, Wyoming, in 1960, the bathroom in the hallway was normal. It contained a tub, a toilet, a sink – all in white porcelain – and a small vanity with a set of slim drawers and a cupboard underneath. The toilet paper and bathtub soap were the first things to go in, and for about twenty-four hours, the room served the primary function for which it was created. But once the bags were unpacked and we really started to settle in, the tiny room underwent a conversion – it became my mother's bathroom.

I could still use it for its intended purpose, as long as I acknowledged in my heart that it had actually risen above all that with the introduction of my mother's stuff. It had gone from function to fashion, from a black-and-white snapshot in a family album to a full-page, full-color glossy advertisement in *Vogue*. More skilled than any home decorator, my mother had caused that transformation just by unpacking her beauty case.

A casual observer might have mistaken it all for a collection of makeup and skin-care products, but that person would have been wrong. It was, in fact, the essence of womanhood – female beauty stripped down to its DNA. My mother, of course, was the most fascinating and beautiful female I knew, but I had been exposed to many others, mostly through the after-dinner world inside our black-and-white Zenith TV, and since I knew I was one of their tribe, I was keeping a close eye on just exactly how they handled things.

The commercials on television were perfect, although colorless, representations of real life. The families looked like ours – white and middle class, with a mother and a father and at least one child all living in a home that was clean but could be cleaner, wearing whites that could be whiter, and eating food that was good but could be better. And my mother was representative of what I would eventually become – an adult woman, a wife, and a mother, one who looked good but could be new and improved with just a spritz of perfume, a smear of blue eye shadow, and a perfectly applied set of ruby-red lips.

Adult women inhabited a space that was fraught with difficulty – dirty rings on collars and in toilet bowls, hair that wouldn't comb through, grass stains on pant knees, and rice that wasn't fluffy – and they always managed to solve the problem. But more than that, they always looked good doing it. The behind-the-scenes work that it took – what I witnessed in my mother's bathroom – made sense on some primal level. This was what a woman had to do to prepare for all the tragedies that she was going to face as soon as she left the safety of the bathroom, and even more importantly, to find a man who would help her get through it all – someone like Ward Cleaver or Rob Petrie or Ken.

And my mother was my guide to this future, much as I assumed my Barbie was to Skipper. She would teach me the ways of womanhood. In the one-room schoolhouse that was her bathroom, I had already learned that lips could be pink or red or something called "mauve." Eyelids could be brown or green or blue. Amazingly, they could also be "mauve." And although greasy faces smeared with beauty cream were acceptable when there was only housework to be done, shiny noses were a major breach of etiquette. And then there was the hair.

Blonde hair was not a luxury. It was the mark of a beautiful woman. The only women who could truly get away with not being blonde were Laura Petrie and Jackie Kennedy – but they had other assets that carried them, like being married to handsome, successful men. My mother was naturally blonde, but I discovered that this, too, could be enhanced. There was a thing called frosting that wasn't pertinent to cakes, and it made blonde hair blonder.

My mother's monthly ritual involved pulling on a plastic cap, attacking her head with what appeared to be knitting needles, and pulling tiny strands of hair through the holes in the cap. Pieces of hair stuck out of her head on all sides, leaving her looking like a baby willow tree. Then the stinky white "frosting" went on the strands. This was best accomplished while a cigarette burned in a plastic ashtray on the vanity, so when I watched, I could breathe in second-hand smoke and peroxide at the same time, unknowingly preparing my brain for college drug experimentation and my future nicotine habit.

When everything was over, the cigarette got hoisted to her mouth and I got to watch her inhale and exhale, curls of smoke from the tip wafting toward me on invisible peroxide fumes, eventually mingling with the warm, gray cloud of her exhalation. The elegance of the entire sequence of gestures gave the whole glamorizing process that I was witnessing an air of mystery and sophistication. The small bathroom suddenly became a dressing room and my mother a movie star – or Miss America – waiting to be called onto the stage.

That I wasn't completely grounded in reality had more to do with the chatter coming in from outside – the radio, the television, the magazines my mother got, the books I read, the Disney movies that I got to see – than with any mental pathology. I was simply trying to sort through it all and figure out what was important. I needed to latch onto a thread of something that I could follow to completion, because people – adults – were already starting to ask me what I wanted to be when I grew up, in a time when you picked something and then became that, in a time when children were already supposed to have a handle on these things. And watching my mother day in and day out, examining the tools of her trade there in the hallway bathroom, huffing peroxide at least once a month when she frosted her hair, I finally formulated my answer: "Beautiful."

It seemed like a worthy goal, especially with cash, cars, and college scholarships in the offing. Thanks to the Miss America pageant, everyone in the country was well aware of the lucrative results of being beautiful, and I was pretty sure that everyone cared as much as I did. For me, it was more than just entertainment. It was serious, something to study and learn from, much like television commercials.

On that special night, my mother and I arranged our Big Chief tablets and pencils on the TV trays in front of us, careful not to tip over our popcorn bowls. We were ready to track our favorites and see how close we came to the decisions of the judges, who couldn't possibly know more about beauty than my mother did.

In the meantime, my father, filled with his own antici-pation, stretched out on the couch and opened the evening paper, blocking the entire upper half of his body from our view. The television was almost warmed up, and I wriggled with anticipation. On the darkened screen, a picture suddenly burst forth, and Bert Parks' brilliant white smile appeared on the screen.

"There she is, Miss America. There she is, your ideal," he sang as the women paraded across the stage. Even in black and white, they were radiant, and each was undoubtedly the most beautiful woman in her state. How difficult it must have been for those other women at home watching, the ones who might have been second or third most beautiful. And it was probably even tougher for those who were down towards the bottom of the beauty rankings in their respective states – say, the two-millionth most beautiful. The fact that not every young woman in the country aspired to the title would have been a huge surprise to me – and I would have felt a little sorry for the ones who didn't. To miss out on one of the most authenticating rituals in life by choice? Unthinkable.

As each woman paraded across the stage, my mother and I formed our assessments and made our selections.

"Miss California," I said, as wise as any of the judges. "She's the best. She's blonde."

"Oh, but those thighs," my mother said. "I don't know."

Her frosted hair sparkled in the glow of the pole lamp like she was wearing her own personal tiara, and she pinched the skin of her throat as she often did when she was confused or thinking hard. I didn't realize that she was playing the game, making the whole thing seem as if each woman's future depended on what we, there in our living room, decided. I took her concern to be legitimate.

"She plays the accordion really well," I countered, but I was already convinced that Miss California's thighs were huge and monstrous things.

"Well, yes, she does, but … the accordion? What about that baton twirler? Who was that?"

I consulted my notes. "Miss Arkansas. But you could twirl a baton better than that, Mom. When you were a majorette, remember?"

My mother shrugged. "Not with fire, though."

"Well, what about the tap dancer?"

"We really should be rooting for Miss Wyoming," my mother cautioned, as if our living room were bugged. And it was possible, given the fact that the Russians were sneaky and stealthy and would probably have done anything they could to sabotage this patriotic display of Americanism.

"Do any of these women have any talent?" My father poked his head over the top of his newspaper long enough to frown at the screen.

"Well, that's not what it's about," I said.

And I knew for certain that it wasn't about talent, and any attempt by the announcers, the sponsors, or the pageant itself to pretend that it was anything less than a bow to the sheer beauty of women was misguided at best. My poor naïve father actually seemed to believe that there were other assets that mattered. Miss California could play her accordion until her fingers fell off and it would never make up for the tree trunks she called thighs.

I rolled my eyes and turned back to my paperwork. "Okay, Miss Wyoming might be all right, but which one is perfect?"

My mother and I spent the rest of the evening scribbling furiously on our pads and cheering or booing as each candidate was selected to move on or was eliminated, often leaving the stage in tears. Miss California always ended up in the top five, no matter how wobbly and cumbersome her thighs, and even if my favorite wasn't chosen, I swelled with emotion at the sheer grandness of it all. The new Miss America's tears of joy were a powerful testament to the importance of the whole affair.

She was Miss America. She was our ideal.

The Naked Truth

MY MOTHER'S BEST friend was constantly recounting the story of my mother's falsies coming loose and floating to the top of the pool when they all went for a swim in college. I had heard that story beginning at age four, but it had bounced around in my head for a couple of years with nothing to latch onto that would give it any meaning.

Then *Playboy* arrived in our home, and the unanchored tale was suddenly given a context. It was an "ah-hah" moment for my six-year-old self, and one that very quickly took on the trappings of "normal" rather than "disturbing," since my mother let me peruse *Playboy* as freely as I did *Life* and *Ladies' Home Journal*, both of which dulled in comparison to this new and exotic discovery.

By the time *Playboy* showed up in the mailbox, I had already learned that we were all supposed to keep our clothes on when we weren't in the bathtub. It was more than a family tradition – it seemed to apply to the whole world. So I was not only baffled by the naked women in the magazine, but by the fact that my mother appeared unconcerned about their nudity and about me seeing it.

"They're naked," I said when I first opened the magazine's glossy, full-color pages.

My mother shrugged. "Well, yes, honey, but mostly just the top part."

My eyes scanned the pages, taking in the bouffant-haired women who, for some reason, washed their cars and went camping without their shirts.

"Why?" I asked, studying them more intently.

"It's a magazine for men," my mother said, as if that were explanation enough.

And apparently it was. This magazine for men suddenly seemed natural and normal, something that my teacher probably had in her house for her husband, something that would make perfect sense for men to read. I didn't fully grasp the *reason* that men might want to read it, but I thought that it might have something to do with the reason that I liked to watch Mike, the neighbor boy, pee around the side of his house where nobody else could see. I wanted to see what he "had," and it was fascinating to watch what he had making an arching yellow stream across the lawn, purely for my enjoyment.

Along those same lines, men probably wanted to see what women "had" as well, and they obviously had to buy a magazine to find this out. My father was certainly going to be in the know when he got a look at *Playboy*.

My mother had bought the magazine subscription as a gift for him, but she seemed far more interested in it than he did. My parents lived in parallel universes, both moving along through life together, connected somewhere, like conjoined twins, by their mutual adoration. But while beauty ruled my mother's universe, brains ruled my father's. Miss May would have only held his interest if she were posed next to her Harvard diploma.

It wasn't that my father didn't appreciate beauty. He had seen my mother's right away. But he also believed that she was smarter than he was, which mightily impressed him, since he was fairly intelligent himself. These two simple concepts – my mother's intelligence and my father's admiration of it – were beyond the scope of my childhood understanding. Brains didn't show – beauty did. The tangible things commanded my attention and were far more easily absorbed. Thank goodness that in my mother's universe, where I spent most of my time, Avon and *Playboy* ruled.

The women of *Playboy* immediately became new role models for me – ultra glamorous, just like my mother and Miss America, but with something percolating below the surface, something naughty in a pleasant way, something just as powerful as beauty, maybe more so. And I sensed that this something was mine for the taking as soon as I truly learned how to use my womanly charms. Exuding this sexual undercurrent while looking really good and keeping my toilet bowl clean was simply another part of the responsibility that I would be taking on as an adult female. I was to have breasts and to use them wisely and often in my pursuit of fame, admiration, and most of all, a man.

My own chest looked nothing like what I saw in *Playboy*, but I was sure that it was only a matter of time before my breasts became round and firm, swelling out of a tiny bikini top or a black lace bra. Then I could take my top off and wash the car in the driveway while the neighborhood men looked on in awe. I had no idea what my father might think of such an activity, but judging by the fact that there was a magazine giving reverence to such things, I assumed that he would be mighty proud.

That none of these women would be deemed worthy of becoming Miss America because of her sordid history in the media never occurred to me. They all seemed wonderful enough to wear the crown. Being in *Playboy* suddenly became my new goal. I would start there and work my way up to Miss America.

After carefully examining every page, I snuck into my

mother's bathroom and closed the door. Then I took off my shirt, turning from side to side, jutting out my nonexistent chest and sucking in my shapeless stomach, bending at the waist to laugh over my naked shoulder and raising my arms above my head to highlight my torso. Looking at my reflection over the growing collection of beauty products lining the vanity, I decided that it was this – this body and this casual, carefree way of displaying it – that would get me what I wanted in life, beginning with the husband that seemed to lurk around the edges of every grown-up woman's life like a bland but necessary accessory.

It was starting to come together. And it was shortly after being introduced to *Playboy* that I began to wear my mother's half-slip in pursuit of my own glamour. There was still that little conflict between general nakedness and social acceptability in my neighborhood, regardless of what was going on in the magazines, so I couldn't run around without my clothes. But my mother had a pale blue half-slip that she let me use for playing dress up, and when I pulled it up under my arms, it made the perfect strapless evening gown.

My mother had something similar in her "go-to-hell" dress, a form-fitting, bright red strapless sheath that took a lot of her energy to wriggle into, but that seemed to epitomize both the sex and the glamour that I had seen in *Playboy*. And my father liked it, which I understood to be the goal. So I set about to find my own "husband" in my strapless blue gown.

I tried things out on my father, mostly because he was in very close proximity and he was ultimately safe. It all began innocently enough, while he was relaxing in his easy chair one night in front of the television, an unsuspecting target of the newfound sexual knowledge that I had gleaned from the pages of *his* magazine. Seeing him so relaxed and open to new experiences, I donned my blue gown, slithered into his lap, and began to wriggle like a garter snake in a tacky imitation of an actress I had seen on television.

"Oh, Daddy. Daddy," I said, doing my best to emulate the writhing actress who, thankfully, had actually said "Oh, Donald."

My mother, who was smoking a cigarette and reading the paper on the couch nearby, raised her eyebrows to look over the tops of her reading glasses, then gave an amused smirk, which told me that I was being adorable and that I should continue. My father, only wanting his lap clear and his freedom back, smiled wanly and gave out a half-hearted sigh, which served to encourage me.

"Oooh, Daaaaddy," I went on, shimmying my shoulders against his chest and trying to wrap my arms around his neck. "I looove you, Daddy." I had now insinuated my entire undulating self between my father and the television screen, and although he wasn't irritated, he seemed a little wriggly himself.

"Jenny," he finally said, attempting and failing to hold me at arm's length, since I was not only six years old but particularly slippery in my satin evening gown. "You need to get off, honey."

"But, Daaaddy," I said, moving my lips close to his ear. "I looove you."

He cleared his throat. "Yes, well, I need to get a candy bar."

I stopped wiggling then, feeling the first little pinprick of rejection. "Mom can get it for you."

My mother looked over, raised her eyebrows again, and went back to her newspaper.

"Your mother's not my maid," he said. "I'm going to get it myself."

And with that, he raised himself gently, so I slid down and hit the floor with only a moderate thump. It wasn't painful, but the rebuff of his retreating back was, and I crossed my arms and glowered.

I had no evidence, but I had a vague idea that if my mother had done the same thing, she would not have ended up sitting on the carpet alone. Donald certainly hadn't rejected the woman on television in such a rude manner. In fact, he had fallen into her waiting feminine arms. But I soothed my bruised ego – and my bruised behind – with the knowledge that it was really only an experiment. My father was already taken. I was merely working my way up to my real goal.

Billy was eight, and there were several reasons why he became my first crush – he lived next door for easy access, his sister Marie was my friend, and he was the only boy I knew well besides those in school, where I could never have gotten away with wearing my gown. So I waited until Saturday night, when Marie's parents came over to play cards with Marie in tow. Marie's teenaged sisters would be out on dates, which meant that Billy would be home alone. As soon as they arrived, I dragged Marie into my room and closed the door.

"I'm going to put on my evening gown and go see Billy," I announced.

Marie, at five, was a year younger than I was and had light brown hair, pale skin, and a tiny and delicate face. When she was utterly repulsed, she had a way of twisting her mouth and squinting her eyes so that it looked as if she was getting ready to throw up.

"Why do you want to do that?"

"I want him to be my boyfriend."

"Well, I don't think he will."

"He will when he sees me in this." I slipped out of my pedal pushers and blouse and pulled on the half-slip. "See?" I wiggled my bare shoulders and took a few prancing steps around the room, doing my best imitation of the Miss America contestants in the evening gown competition.

Marie shook her head. "I don't know. He doesn't really like girls."

"He will when he sees me in this."

She made the face again. "Why should that make a difference?"

I looked at her as if she had questioned the importance of eyeliner. But then I remembered how very young she was. She didn't have the secret knowledge that I had.

I lowered my voice and leaned toward her. "Okay," I said. "Come on. I'll show you."

I opened the door a crack and peeked out. In the distance, I could hear adult voices transformed by alcohol and the excitement of Saturday-night cards. We were safe. I motioned to Marie and we slipped out the crack in the door rather than opening it all the way, just to make things a little more dramatic, and then we tiptoed across the hall to my parents' bedroom. The room was darkened, but the door was open, which meant that it was actually okay to go in, spoiling some of the thrill of the moment. But the fact that my parents wouldn't approve of this mission made it a dangerous one.

When we arrived, I turned on the light and dug into their wicker magazine basket until I produced the proof that Billy would go crazy over my half-naked body displayed in a strapless gown.

"Oh, my stars," Marie said, copying something she had heard both our mothers say. "Where are their clothes?"

I shrugged. "They took them off."

"But why?"

"It's a magazine for men," I said with a superior air. I knew all about this. Marie was just learning. I had to be patient.

"Oh," Marie said, nodding as she flipped through the glossy pages. "Okay."

"And this is what men like," I explained, first pointing at the centerfold that Marie had stretched out on my parents' bed, then pointing to myself in my revealing gown.

"Oh," Marie said again, as if she wasn't quite sure I was telling her the truth.

But I was.

Marie was as spellbound by the magazine as I had been when I first discovered it, and she refused to put it away, even when I insisted that it was time to go next door and present my half-naked self to her brother.

"I can't believe these women are naked," she kept saying as she carefully turned the pages forward and back again. "Look at her. Look at her."

"I know, I know, I've seen them all. Let's go."

"Let's take this and show Billy," she suggested.

"No," I said, stomping my foot. "He only gets to see me." I knew instinctively that if Billy got a look at that magazine, I didn't stand a chance. I snatched it away from her and put it back in the basket. "Let's go."

As we edged down the hall, I could hear our parents laughing in the dining room, their voices getting louder as they switched from my father's homemade beer to his homemade Japanese sake. It was easy to slip out the sliding glass door and follow the moonlight across the backyard to Marie's house, where Billy sat in the darkened living room watching *Zorro* or *Gunsmoke* or some other ridiculous show that the networks had to put on to please boys who had never seen *Playboy* and didn't know any better.

I hid in the kitchen, just a few feet away, as Marie burst into the living room, situated herself between Billy and the television set, and cried out, "Presenting ... the girl of your dreams."

That was my cue. I strode into the spotlight of the television screen, turning this way and that to allow Billy to admire me from all sides, doing my best to imitate a *Playboy* model, Miss America, and my mother in her "go-to-hell" dress all at once. At first, he appeared awestruck. He simply stared, which I considered a positive reaction. Then he stood up and began to walk toward me.

I wasn't sure what would happen, but I had seen my parents kiss before my father left for work, a smacking of lips together like the click of magnets, and I readied myself for this possibility by puckering up. In an instant, Billy was in front of me and I waited for contact. I could see his hand reaching toward me, I could feel it grasping my gown, and in a flash, the half-slip was down around my waist and my most precious commodity, however small, was revealed in the flickering glow of weekly action-adventure.

"Now get out of my way," Billy said. "I'm trying to watch the show."

For a moment, I stood in motionless disbelief over what had just happened. Billy wasn't playing by any rules that I had learned. In my fairy tales, the prince always wanted to kiss the princess well before disrobing her, a part we never got to see anyway. The men in my mother's soap operas were all over the beautiful women in their gowns. And Barbie always got her man, even if I had to make up the story.

I had been prepared for anything, as long as it involved

velvety purple sunsets, happily ever afters, and the promise of relief from household drudgery. But I had not been prepared for this. And when the reality of my rejection finally hit, I burst into tears, yanking the slip back up as I struggled to get out of the house.

"You don't have anything anyway," Billy called to my retreating back.

That remark stung more than my rejection, more than my violation. I had nothing. How was I ever going to get by in the world? I stormed through the back door, sobbing loudly enough to disrupt the drunken card game.

"What's wrong?" my mother called from the dining room.

Since she hadn't bothered to get up, I stomped into the dining room and blurted out, "Billy pulled my gown down like this." And then I did it myself, yanking on the half-slip until it fell to my waist. Among the grownups there was a moment of shocked silence, and then a ball of laughter exploded over the table and rushed toward me, surrounding me and my pathetic naked torso. Ignoring Marie, who had helplessly followed me back from her house, I went to my room and slammed the door.

I didn't measure up. All the hard study that I had undertaken, observing my mother in her bathroom, watching the Miss America pageant as closely as I watched the good citizenship films we were shown in school, studying *Playboy* as if it were an encyclopedia – none of it was paying off. There was no way I was doing all this for nothing.

There had to be some way around it, and time was on my side. After all, this was America. I was certain that the people in charge of it all would never present a goal that would be impossible to achieve. Any boy could be president – that was certain. And any girl could get her man.

The Disappearance of Richard

IDON'T KNOW HOW the game got started, but one night it just did. It didn't strike me as unnatural and probably never would have had I not eventually moved from the world of a seven-year-old girl into a grownup system of gender and sexuality that didn't approve of bending the rules. The game that Toby and I played seemed almost normal – a game of pretend. And maybe it *was* normal. Maybe it was everything else that was suspect.

Toby was a girl, and that was obvious – at least if you looked close enough. She already had the beginnings of breasts at nine years old, and she didn't have a penis. I knew this because we often took baths together when I spent the night at her house. But she wasn't like any of the other girls I knew in 1962 – the girls at school or in my Brownie troop.

Those girls ran screaming from spiders and worms, wore dresses to birthday parties, and served high tea to their dolls. I did these things, too. It was these little-girl activities, more than the lack of a penis or the expectation of breasts, that defined us as girls. Toby was the only one I knew who needed to present anatomical clues so I could nail down her gender. She was different.

Toby was two years older than me, big and broad-shouldered, with a spray of nutmeg-colored freckles across her nose. One canine tooth sat crooked in her mouth, so that it was the first thing anyone saw when she smiled. Her cropped hair was more beige than brown or blonde, and she didn't seem to care much which direction it went when it decided to go somewhere. Over the three years that she befriended me, she owned two dogs, two salamanders, a guinea pig, a hamster, four chickens, a snake, and an iguana.

She took in neighborhood strays and I was one of them, trying to find my home among the ballerina paintings on my bedroom wall and the various Barbie dolls that were strewn about the floor among a sea of fashionable clothing and accessories. I knew what beautiful was supposed to be, and I knew what a girl was supposed to be, and Toby wasn't exactly either one of those things. But she was the most beautiful girl I knew.

Toby loved *The Twilight Zone*, and since I idolized Toby, I loved it, too. The only difference was that Toby could watch the entire "Talky Tina" episode without flinching, while I ran shrieking from the room as soon as the evil doll told Telly Savalas that she hated him. I couldn't look at Chatty Cathy for a week. But Toby lived on fear. She sucked it up through the shows she watched and the books she read, and then spit it back out whole on our sleepovers.

"A man was on vacation in California," she told me as we huddled beneath the covers in her bedroom. "And he went into the ocean for a swim. When he came out, he saw a little piece of sponge attached to his leg. He pulled on it, but it wouldn't come off. He didn't think anything about it, though, and he went back into the ocean. And when he came out ..." She paused dramatically and I could feel her eyes widen and her face contort, even though the room was too dark to make out her features. "... he was covered from head to toe. He was just one ... big ... sponge."

I shivered under the blankets and vowed that I would never swim in the ocean, because the story, of course, was true. Everything Toby told me was true. She knew more about life than I could ever hope to. She had read every *Superman* comic ever written, watched every episode of *The Twilight Zone* and *The Outer Limits* without getting scared, and liked to look at books containing actual photographs of soldiers being blown to bits in World War II. For some reason, her father collected these books and didn't seem to mind the children simply browsing through them as if they were *Highlights* magazines. Toby thrived on them – the bloodier, the better. I doubted that she had ever picked up a *Highlights* magazine in her life.

At Toby's house, I would lie on the bed while she read *The Rime of the Ancient Mariner* or *The Pit and the Pendulum* out loud. On Halloween, Toby was a zombie with a plastic hatchet in her chest, white painted hair and blue lips, and I loped along behind her down child-infested streets, pulling my coat around me to hide my stupid fairy princess costume. On the windiest, coldest days of the year, we took a little Sterno camping cooker onto the prairie that bordered our neighborhood and roasted hot dogs until the skins turned dark green and cracked, while Toby matter-of-factly discussed the snakes that were no doubt all around us. And, oh, how she told stories.

"There was a girl who wanted a dog."

I was still quaking from the spongeman, but I listened carefully to the Vincent-Price voice that rose from the bottom of her throat.

"But her father wouldn't let her have one, so he bought her a stuffed dog. But she still wanted a real one. Then, one day, she went into the kitchen and got a knife. And her father saw her going into her bedroom with the knife and the stuffed dog and her chemistry set."

I stiffened and sucked in my breath.

"She was in there for a long time, and then her father heard strange noises coming from the bedroom. So he went down the hall and opened the door and ..."

I chewed on my bottom lip and closed my eyes, waiting for the hideous conclusion.

"What ... did ... the ... father ... see?" she said, drawing out each word until it stood by itself.

"I don't know," I hissed. "What did he see?"

I could feel the covers move as she shrugged. "That's the moral of the story," she said. "What did the father see?"

I let out my breath in disappointment. I actually knew what a moral was and how it figured into a story, and "What did the father see?" was in no way a moral to any kind of story. But I wasn't about to explain that to Toby. If she said it was a moral, it was a moral, and I never did find out what the father saw. I could only imagine his disgust and terror at whatever it was. It didn't really matter that Toby's definitions were different from everyone else's, because she was everything she wasn't supposed to be.

By that time, I already knew what girls were supposed to do and what boys were supposed to do. Boys were supposed to read *Superman* comics, while girls read *Archie* or *Little LuLu*. Boys were supposed to own iguanas and snakes, and girls were supposed to run from them. Boys were supposed to scare girls with spooky campfire stories about sponge-men or maniacal little girls and their stuffed dogs. Boys read Edgar Allan Poe, if they read at all, and girls read Laura Ingalls Wilder. But *Little House on the Prairie* could never hold its own against *The Tell-Tale Heart* if Toby were doing the choosing. She was wild and reckless and not of this world, and I was crazy in love with her – especially when we played the game.

"Would you like some wine, dear?" Toby held her Coke bottle out for me to examine. She was well versed in the ways of alcohol, since her parents drank it with abandon. Her parents also slept in the nude and were Republicans, which seemed exotic and otherworldly. But their drinking habits and their lack of clothing assured that Toby and I would not be disturbed behind the closed doors of her bedroom after the household had turned in for the night.

"I think I will," I replied, shyly offering my plastic tumbler while I pulled my cocktail dress, which was really Toby's nightgown, tighter around my shoulders.

"It's sherry," Toby pointed out. "Like your name."

My name was always Sherry when we played this game.

Then Toby approached with the "wine," pouring it effortlessly into my glass while holding my chin in her hand so she could gaze into my eyes and tell me how lovely I looked tonight. She adjusted her smoking jacket, which was really her brother's bathrobe, and we both sat down on the black leather couch, which was really the edge of Toby's bed.

"Why, thank you, Richard," I said, fluttering my eyelashes and pressing a hand to my chest.

Toby's name was always Richard when we played this game.

After we were both settled, side by side, we laughed and chatted and clinked our tumblers together in an imitation of the toasts we had seen at grownup parties. We were grownups, too, in this game, emulating the world in which we lived and carrying out the roles that we had seen, as all children do, but with one small discrepancy – I was preparing for my real future as a woman. Toby was preparing for some impossible, fantasy future as a man.

As Richard and Sherry, we could spend the entire evening

discussing the significance of the "Room for One More"
episode of *The Twilight Zone* or why Little Jackie Paper eventually left Puff the Magic Dragon or what would happen when
the Martians finally made it down to Earth. Sometimes we
reviewed the rivalry between Lois Lane and Lana Lang, and
other times we examined our hypothesis that Clark Kent was
actually better looking than Superman. Occasionally, we talked about the merits of Miss Grundy versus Mr. Weatherbee or
why Betty was really superior to Veronica. We were still children, just playing at a grownup game, so it was all perfectly
acceptable – or maybe not.

There was already some small seed of a thought, germinat-
ing somewhere underneath it all, that we shouldn't get caught
– that this was something that the real grownups might not fully
appreciate. But we weren't quite sure why, and we didn't really
want to know. We just wanted to keep playing the game.

"I don't understand," Richard said, pouring more wine
and looking deep into my eyes, "why Lois and Lana are constantly fighting over Superman. Clark Kent is so much more
handsome and intelligent looking in those glasses, don't you
agree?"

"Oh, yes, Richard," I cooed, wriggling my shoulders. "But
not nearly as handsome as you."

"Well, we can drink to that," Richard said, and we raised
our tumblers in a toast to Richard's attractiveness.

Once during the game, Richard kissed me – or rather, he
kissed Sherry – in a flat, pressed way, outer lips upon outer
lips, and then he smiled seductively without revealing the
crooked canine. Although the kiss was unimpressive, it didn't
seem wrong, because even though I had an idea that girls
didn't kiss each other, it wasn't Toby who had kissed me.
There was no Toby when Richard was in the room.

And the fact that Toby was lost so completely made the game that much more exciting – and that much more normal. We were a woman and a man, partaking of women and men things in the privacy of Toby's bedroom. What – and who – we would be when we left there was of no consequence. The only world that was real was the one inside that room.

The game lasted until my family moved away. I didn't see Toby again until I was twelve and she was fourteen. When I found out that she was coming to visit for a week, I pictured frog hunts at the creek, ghost stories at midnight, and the two of us perusing the comic book racks for the latest issue of *Superman*. I pictured Richard floating toward me across the crowded bus terminal in his smoking jacket, ready to return to the romance that had been so cruelly thwarted by the thoughtless decisions of real adults.

Instead, the girl who finally materialized from the crowd looked as if she had just stepped out of the pages of *Seventeen for the Full-Figured Girl*. Toby had boobs and hips and thickly lined eyes. Dressed in a psychedelic orange minidress and sporting a cropped and frosted "Twiggy" haircut, Toby was almost unrecognizable as the girl/man who had once offered me sherry from a Coke bottle and raved about my imaginary beauty. As I examined her, my stomach twisted at the knowledge that she would never again own, or even touch, a snake.

Toby had turned into someone who read teen fashion magazines, wore makeup, and worried about her weight and how she looked. She had turned into someone who recognized the larger scheme of things in the world and had willingly accepted her place – a pre-*Stepford Wives* representation of young womanhood. Richard had vanished without so much as a fingerprint left behind, and it was obvious that he was never coming back.

Toby taught me how to wear makeup that week. Toby showed

me what was important to look at – and to buy – in the teen fashion magazines. It was Toby who mentored me as I struggled into the world of clothes, cosmetics, and body consciousness that my impending adolescence was suddenly requiring. This girl who had once stretched out on the floor with her iguana as if it were a snuggly kitten, who could recite from memory the life history of every villain who had ever threatened Superman, who sat up after dark hoping that the Abominable Snowman would appear outside her bedroom window, had fought nobly on the battleground of the gender frontier and had either lost or won, depending on your point of view.

Looking back, I sometimes feel as if the culture reined in Toby like a cowboy ropes a wild bull, but I could be dead wrong. Maybe Toby really wanted to wear psychedelic mini-skirts and black eyeliner and flavored lip gloss. Maybe she didn't want to have pet iguanas anymore. Maybe she had out-grown *Superman* comics, and maybe *Seventeen* and *Vogue* and *Glamour* magazines rang true to her.

It's possible that the space in which she lived was the result of a conscious and informed decision. Since my own transi-tion, I've come to realize that acceptance of a truly authentic spirit has to encompass all possible permutations, and Toby's decisions about herself might not have been influenced by anything but her own desire to be who she really was. If that's the case, then Toby should have been exactly as she appeared when I saw her at the bus station. The real Toby had finally materialized.

But if underneath the layers of mascara and the high-fash-ion haircut there was someone longing for the sting of prairie sand pelting her face in the wind, for the feel of a snake wrig-gling against her arm, for the dry press of Sherry's lips against her own, then something went terribly wrong.

I'll never know. I only saw Toby once after that visit. We were both adult women then, and we talked about the things that adult women sometimes talk about – relationships, careers, how we got where we were, and where we might go from there. We talked about trying to find the "right" man, and we compared our string of alcoholic, drug-addicted, or unemployed boyfriends and our abusive ex-husbands – the ongoing sagas of our lives.

I never asked her what became of Richard – whether he was dead or simply buried alive under the rubble of expectations that had collapsed in on her when it was time to grow up. I don't know if things might have been different for her had she been born in a different time and place – maybe now, when she would have other role models to choose from and other paths more available to her. She went her way and I went mine, and we completely lost touch, never to recover it.

Maybe she finally met the "right" man and settled down to vote Republican and sleep in the nude while her children played their own games behind closed bedroom doors. Or maybe she didn't need to meet the right man. Maybe he was there all along.

Boy Attacks

JANICE PERRY WASN'T really a friend. She lived across the street and had a tetherball set that hooked right into a deep hole in her driveway. When she wanted to play, she would go outside and set up the tetherball, then bat the ball around until one of the neighborhood kids saw her and decided to join in.

Even with her short stature and wiry arms, she was a tetherball wizard, and she always welcomed me when I hesitantly crossed the street, because she knew she could beat me consistently within a couple of minutes. We could play up to thirty games of tetherball in an hour, with me flailing my arms in the air as the ball passed by or reaching up to protect my face while Janice walloped the ball over and over until the cord was completely wound around the pole. I never knew when that happened, because my hands were always over my eyes.

I had grown fat in the last couple of years, and clumsy, and unattractive, with hair that was both stringy and stiff, much like a used Brillo pad, and sticking out in all directions. There was no longer any hope for the Miss America title or for the possibility of a latent beauty gene inherited from my mother. It was obvious that something had gone awry. But that little genetic mishap was nothing compared with what was to come.

Janice's older brother, Greg, was someone I had seen before but never noticed. He was fourteen and was usually off on his bike somewhere doing whatever it was that boys did when they careened out of their driveway and disappeared down the street. I was always too busy concentrating on keeping my nose from a lethal collision with the tetherball to pay much attention to the goings-on of the rest of Janice's family. But suddenly, something was different.

That Greg had abruptly appeared in my field of vision was not so much of a surprise. I was ten, and puberty had already begun, inching its way, little by little, into my life, so smooth and stealthy that I hadn't even realized the damage until it was too late.

Greg was thin, like Janice, but tall, with sandy hair that fell across his forehead and into his eyes when he readied himself on his bike. Once in a while, he would stick his lanky arm up and stop the tetherball in mid flight, annoying Janice but giving me enough of a reprieve that I could pull my hands away from my face and look at him. That's when I could see the too-big nose centered in his angular face, the small, ropy muscles straining in his forearms as he gripped the bike handles, and the random placement of whiskers, like a brush with missing bristles, across his chin and along his jawline.

"Gre-eg," Janice would whine. "Stop messing up the game. I was winning."

She would say this as if it had been her one chance to beat me.

Then Greg would laugh and say, "It's a stupid game," in a voice that crackled like a short-wave radio. And he would ride off down the street, hunched over a bike that was already too small for him, as I watched his back disappear into the neighborhood.

And the reality that dawned on me as I watched him ride away was that I wanted to *be* Greg Perry – more than anything else in the world. And this made me decide that I must be in love with him. Not only must I be in love with him, but I no doubt loved him more than any girl had ever loved another boy in the history of the world – that was probably why I wanted to be him.

My mother loved my father, I was pretty sure, but she had never once talked about wanting to be him. I had seen Disney movies where teenaged starlets fell in love with the men they met, and Cinderella and Sleeping Beauty fell in love with their princes. But none of them ever said that they wanted to *be* that man or that prince. They all seemed perfectly satisfied simply being the object of male affection. Therefore my love for Greg Perry must have been just that much stronger. It was so strong that it lasted all the way up until the time that my parents took me to see *A Midsummer Night's Dream* at the Lincoln Community Playhouse in Lincoln, Nebraska, where we now lived. That's when I fell in love with the man who played Puck.

He was probably only sixteen or seventeen, but I thought he was a man, because he was on stage and commanded attention. He looked like Greg Perry, only better – older and more seasoned, like a true Shakespearean actor. When Puck was on stage, the rest of the cast might as well have taken a break, because I was watching only him, and from the minor stirs among the other young female audience members whenever he appeared, it seemed that I was not alone.

Afterward, I waited in line for twenty minutes just to get him to sign my program. The autographing was taking place outside on the lawn, and Puck was squatted down in the grass among his throng of fans, most of them giggling preteen girls, gently taking each program and scribbling his name across the front. I watched him through the dimming evening light, the shadows falling across his face from his jaunty pointed hat.

I practiced what I would say to him when I finally got my turn. *Good job,* I would say, casual in my appraisal so he wouldn't think me forward, but with enough true feeling that he would take notice. Or maybe I would say *You were the best one in the show,* adopting the dreamy, cooing voice of Sherry talking to Richard. He would look at me and see beyond the fat and the fact that I was ten years old, and then something would happen. I didn't know what for sure, but it was likely to be one of two things:

His eyes might become starry and distant, with a tiny smile playing at his lips. And then he might stand up and take my hands in his and say, "Jenny, I've been waiting for this moment all my life, which hasn't been that long, but which has certainly felt like it without you." And then I would be transformed, like Cinderella, into a slender blonde with a glittering tiara on my head.

Ignoring the rest of his fans in the line, Puck would pull me over to where my parents waited in the grass and say, "Sir, ma'am, I'd like your daughter's hand in holy matrimony." Of course, my parents would say yes, thinking that another chance like this might never come along in my lifetime, and Puck and I would walk off into the Lincoln sunset to live happily ever after.

Or he might stand up and take my hands and my fingertips would start to disappear into his. Then my arms, my chest, my stomach – all of me would slowly dissolve into the body of Puck and we would meld into one. Then I would *be* Puck, or at least the man who played him, and I would live happily ever after by myself. And, I thought again, that must surely be the truest love that had ever existed – wanting to be the man who played Puck.

When I finally got to the front of the line, Puck looked up, just as I had expected, and I opened my mouth to say whatever fabulously casual comment I had decided on – but no words came out. I simply froze for a moment and then, when my arms started to work again, I shoved my program toward the point in his hat. His thin lips forced a smile, and I saw that his eyes were neither starry nor distant, but exhausted. He was tired – tired of playing Puck, tired of being pleasant to his many adoring fans, tired of his manly responsibilities. Perhaps, even though I couldn't speak, he would see that I held the answers he sought, as he held the answers for me.

I waited. He took my program, like he had all the others, and scribbled his name across the front. Then he handed it back and, when I failed to move, reached around me for the next one. He had moved on.

I left, blindly struggling through the crowd and over to my waiting parents. On the ride home, I cursed myself for failing to speak up and change my life. In my room that night, I cradled my program in my hands, tracing my fingers over the pen marks that were his name, staring at the signature. David Grayson. That was his name. I closed my eyes and swallowed hard and begged the universe to let me be David Grayson. And it was then that I decided on a name for that thing I was feeling, that thing that made me want to be Greg Perry or David Grayson or whatever other boy might come into my field of vision in the future. Love was not nearly a profound enough word – I decided that it must be a boy attack.

My mother was thrilled when I asked to take acting classes at the Lincoln Community Playhouse. I didn't even have to beg. She seemed to hold out hope for everything that came along that might transform me back into what I once was.

After all, actresses were beautiful, they had silky hair, and they weren't fat. But while my mother might have hoped that she would send in a plump, stringy-haired daughter and get back Grace Kelly, I was hoping for another kind of transformation.

Acting classes were in the basement of the Playhouse, which seemed logical to me. We had to start at the bottom before working our way up to the stage. The reality was that, even after the classes, most of us would still be looking at the stage from balcony seating. We would have worked our way right up past the stage and beyond.

Nevertheless, we were an optimistic little group of would-be stars, eight in all, looking to our instructor to make us the toast of the town. Mrs. Sweitser, who was also a director of plays, was a feisty little fireball of a woman with a German accent. I was the oldest and the biggest in my class, both in height and girth, but tiny Mrs. Sweitser was determined that I was going to be a dainty fairy or a graceful, swaying willow tree right along with everyone else. Transformation was her job – which is why, during the fourth class, she brought in a Professional Makeup Artist.

Lady Donna was exotic, magical. Mrs. Sweitser's German accent paled in comparison to that of Lady Donna, who was Russian or Romanian or Czech – or maybe even Transylvanian. She swept into the room, looking to me exactly the way a Professional Makeup Artist should look – petite and compact, with a lavender cape that moved when she did, like a richly colored and eccentric shadow. Her ash-and-white hair, wound around the top of her head, appeared as a chocolate-and-vanilla-swirl ice cream cone. Dynamic, showy, and dripping with Broadway, she had probably spent her life among the dramatic and artsy types that populated the Lincoln community theater scene.

I had waited restlessly for this day ever since Mrs. Sweitser had announced it two weeks before. And when I saw Lady Donna, I was certain that she could take care of everything. If she couldn't do this, no one could.

Lady Donna clapped her hands in the air as she commanded our attention. "Now, my dears," she said, looking around the room with her head held high and her nose slightly raised. "What do you all want to be? Don't be afraid, just tell me, and that is what you shall become."

I yanked at the hems of my poppy-red stretch-cotton shorts. I fussed with the bill of the white vinyl John Lennon cap that my mother had allowed me to purchase, since by that time, I had decided I wanted to be George Harrison – but since George didn't wear a cap, I had to make do with one styled after John's. Of course, my mother wasn't aware of my newly emerging boy attacks, and I hadn't felt the need to discuss them with her. I was still pretty sure that they were a natural byproduct of falling in love, and I didn't want my mother to know that I was falling in love on a regular basis. As displeased as she was with my appearance, she might consider the whole thing hopeless, and I wasn't ready to give up the last remnants of my desire for a real life.

Since I was the oldest in the class, I had to wait until last for Lady Donna's miracles, but the wait would be worth it. Watching patiently as the younger children morphed into clowns or ballerinas or kittens, I bided my time. Finally, she approached me, and I knew that I was on the brink of a major metamorphosis.

"And what is your name, my dear?" she asked, holding my chin in her hand and turning my face this way and that, as if I were merely a canvas that she had been assigned to restore. When I felt her smooth fingertips and smelled the amber of her cologne, I was ready to turn my entire life over to Lady Donna.

"Jennifer," I whispered. It was as if the Holy Spirit had surrounded me and I couldn't speak above a hush.

"Jennifer," she gushed. "What a lovely name. And what do you want to be today, Jennifer?" As she continued to examine my doughy face and the unruly tangle of hair that spilled out from under my cap, she smiled as if everything were completely under control – her control. The impossibility of doing anything with what was in front of her did not seem to occur to her, which made me trust her even more.

"A boy." I wasn't whispering anymore. The pronouncement was so final and so unquestionable that it should have been apparent to all that this was the only answer I could give.

Lady Donna didn't blink. Even in the mid-'60s, someone so worldly was probably used to the occasional gender-bending personality. She simply removed her hand from my face and bent over her greasepaint pots.

"All right," she said. "Today we will make you a boy."

With that, she dipped her fingers into a thick pot of tan-colored paint. "Boys have ruddy complexions. Ruddy," she announced as she rubbed the goo across my face. "Yes, ruddy." She seemed to like the word. It ran smoothly across her lips and tongue.

After I was ruddied up, she swiped a brush across a cake of dark powder and applied it to my eyelids and my cheeks. Then, with a smaller brush, she shaded under my eyes. Finally, she scooped up my mound of hair, stuck it under my cap, tucked a few stray shocks against my head with bobby pins, clasped her hands together, and proclaimed, "Now you are a boy."

And so it was done. I felt a strange and foreign swell in my bones and muscle as my body became male. I sat and talked and walked differently. I only glanced in the hand mirror offered by Lady Donna, pretending that it was reinforcement I didn't need. The truth was that I was secretly afraid. If I looked too hard at myself, I might see through the makeup and discover only myself underneath. If I actually saw Jennifer there, the spell would be broken. If Lady Donna said I was a boy, then I was a boy. That was all the assurance I wanted.

Never mind that I had on red cotton stretch shorts. Never mind that my breasts bulged against my father's castoff shirt. I was so convinced of my maleness that as I sat on the Playhouse steps after class, I knew that the occupants of every passing car saw a boy loitering there, as boys tended to do. Lady Donna, exiting the building with her cases of pots, tubes, and sponges, stopped long enough to compliment her own handiwork.

"If I did not know better," she said, grinning proudly, "I would think you were a boy sitting here."

And I believed her. Of course I was a boy sitting there. I sprawled my legs out and slumped, adopting a casual sneer. This was what it felt like. And it felt good. It felt right. I had truly been transformed. By the time my mother pulled up in our Volkswagen Beetle, I was convinced that she might not recognize me at all. I knew I should have swaggered to the car, but I was too excited. I took off toward our "Bug" at a gallop.

"Mom," I cried as I threw open the car door. "Mom, it's me."

She looked at me and blinked, expressionless, and I thought for a moment that I had been right, that she truly didn't know who I was.

"It's me," I said as I clambered into the car, wiggling my poppy cotton hips into the small space next to her. "Do I look like a boy? Do I look like a boy?"

She now narrowed her eyes and pursed her lips tightly, like she did after applying her lipstick. I thought maybe she was trying to decide. Then she snapped, "Of course not. That's the stupidest thing I've ever heard." And she thrust the car into gear as if the gearshift weighed fifty pounds, and we jolted forward. The entire car was angry.

I slid down into my seat, silent all the way home, still hoping that some driver alongside us at a stoplight might believe that we were mother and son. But my confidence and my sureness were gone. And I also knew that I had disappointed her, even enraged her somehow. This was apparently the last straw. Her ugly, fat daughter had morphed into an ugly, fat son. She had not been prepared for either one. And when we got back to the house, I had to wash my ruddy makeup off. And then I was a girl again – if that's what you called it.

A Period Piece

BECOMING A WOMAN turned out to be the hit film of the sixth grade – at least for the girls. The boys weren't allowed into the gym when this particular blockbuster was being shown. They were all herded into another room, either to watch *Becoming a Man* or the seventh game of the World Series. I never found out, because no boys would talk to me to tell me.

Becoming a Woman was actually a big cartoon with a lot of butterflies and cheerful birds that sailed happily from frame to frame, but it eventually got to the point. When it was all over, I understood that we each had large, smiling eggs inside us that, when united with persistent, animated sperm, would produce a child, and that, when left to their own devices, would disappear monthly, leaving a trail of blood in their wake.

It seemed pretty unpleasant, and it also seemed like new information, although my mother would later say that we had long and detailed talks about it as I was growing up. Mothers were invited to this particular screening, and perhaps what mine remembered as our lengthy discussions was simply her presence in the chair behind me in the gymnasium.

Although no popcorn was served, which was always a disappointment, each girl got a souvenir of her experience – a pink plastic bag with a *Becoming a Woman* booklet, two sanitary pads, and a white elastic belt that looked torturous in its complexity. The whole affair proved to be amazing foresight on the part of the principal, because shortly after that, I found myself sitting on the toilet, staring at an unfamiliar red stain that had materialized on my voluminous pair of white cotton Carters.

It was jolting for a moment – the thought of impending death often is – but I soon realized that this was what *Becoming a Woman* had been talking about. And I really needed the contents of that pink plastic bag, but I wasn't sure what to do with the stuff, because there had been no live-model demonstration at the film, and the instructional drawings in the booklet were as crude as the film animation had been. So I did what I had to do – I called for my mother.

By the time she opened the bathroom door and I displayed the offending underwear, I was visibly shaking as I began to fully comprehend all the ramifications of what was happening. I wasn't sure that I was ready yet to take on the responsibility of "becoming a woman," and I had hoped for some sympathy, but my mother reacted as if I had just produced my first number two in the potty chair.

"Oh, my goodness," she said, clapping her hands together and beaming. "Well, congratulations, Jenny." In an instant, getting my period was transformed into a significant personal achievement, as if I had somehow done something on my own that merited her pride and delight. She was almost giddy as she scurried to my room and returned with the pink plastic bag, digging inside and producing a pad and the intimidating elastic belt.

"Do you know how to use this?" she asked, holding the belt out to me as if it were an award.

I looked at it and shook my head. It looked even more evil now than it had when I had originally taken it out of the sack after the movie. So she showed me how to thread the ends of the pad through the metal clasps and how I was to adjust and wear the belt on my body. She seemed delighted with every aspect of this exercise, but then, she didn't have a metal clasp burrowing painfully between her butt cheeks and an elastic band cutting into the fat around her hips. She was simply overcome by my new womanhood.

This was, apparently, a moment that my mother had been waiting for with desperate optimism. Once I got my period, surely things would change. My hair might automatically straighten and become silky and manageable. I might get a waist that curved inward, or I might at least become less lumpy. I might turn into the daughter that she had always wanted, the one she thought she had before nature took its own course with me. And then maybe she would turn into the daughter that her parents had always wanted, and then maybe her unhappy mother would ... well, it could go on and on, back to our disappointed ancestors. Who knows for sure what a mother's heart hopes for? But she was radiant, as if it were happening to her – or maybe because it wasn't.

"This is the most important thing in a girl's life," she gushed. "This is a big moment for you. This is so exciting."

She went on and on as if she didn't believe I was convinced, and I wasn't. Blood is a scary thing. And according to the *Becoming a Woman* movie, I couldn't even go swimming now, although that might have been a blessing in disguise. The kids at the pool teased me unmercifully when they saw me coming in my one-piece, stretched out on all sides to accommodate the inner tube that I wore *under* my swimming suit. At least now I had an excuse when the neighbor kids all got together for a pool trip. If nothing else, I could sit on the sidelines in a colorful muumuu and pretend to be their chaperone, since I was, after all, a woman.

I went to bed that night swaddled in elastic with a fear of going to school the next day and my mother's words ringing in my ears: "You're going to have to start bathing more frequently now. You have to keep yourself really clean." But even as I lay there considering everything – the pain of the elastic and the clasps, the terror of changing a napkin in the school bathroom, the inevitability of keeping clean, and the paradox of being able to bathe but not go swimming – another round of optimism slowly crept up to the front of my brain. Maybe now that I was a woman, things really would change. Maybe I would wake up and discover that I had another shot at Miss America or *Playboy* after all. Maybe Greg Perry or Puck would return my slightly deranged and obsessive brand of affection.

But as the days went by, I realized that it was not to be. And apparently, so did my mother. A few weeks later, she came home from shopping with a *Seventeen* magazine in one of the brown paper grocery bags.

"It's time you started reading this," she said, smiling gently as she held out the offering, as if she were a stranger trying to lure me into a car. "It's an important magazine for girls your age. You'll get a lot of tips and ideas in here."

I took the glossy magazine into my hands and stared at the cover. Staring back at me was a smiling blonde teenaged girl. As I ran my eyes over the print, I saw that, by reading the magazine, I would learn the new fashion trends for fall, how to talk to boys about what they were interested in, and how to keep my best friend from being jealous of me. Although none of these things seemed to apply in my current state, I went to the kitchen, got a candy bar to fortify me, and then settled on the couch to read the magazine.

My mother, seemingly satisfied that the magazine had captured my attention, retreated to the kitchen to unpack the remainder of the grocery bags, which were filled with luscious items that guaranteed that my best friend would never be jealous of me. When she came out to the living room a few minutes later, she was confronted with a shocking sight.

"How can you go through that so fast?" she said, wide-eyed, her hands on her hips, as if she had suffered a personal affront.

For there I sat, blindly turning the pages of *Seventeen*, trying to figure out exactly what I was supposed to be looking at. What I saw were various advertisements for clothes, a skeletal girl named Twiggy, and pictures of something called "leg makeup" that came in purple and pink and blue and that was apparently applied to the legs in stripes with a miniature paint roller. I was completely bewildered, desperately flipping from one glossy picture to the next while trying to figure out how I could possibly use any of this information.

I looked at my mother in confusion. "What?"

"I said, how can you turn the pages so fast? When I was your age, it took me days to get through a fashion magazine." She intertwined her fingers and put the backs of her hands under her chin, a cross between Eliza Doolittle after she had danced with Henry Higgins and Maria singing about Tony in *West Side Story*. "I used to look at every page and dreeeeeeam of how I would look in the clothes."

I was sure that it must have been easier for someone who could actually fit into the clothes. I saw no "chubby size" offerings, and any dream I could possibly have about being in those outfits would quickly turn into a nightmare as my fat pressed against the seams and split them. But my indifference turned to panic when I realized that my mother actually wanted me to find clothes in the magazine that I might want to buy.

"You'll be going to junior high in a couple of months and

you'll need a new wardrobe," she said. "Look at those models. Don't you want to look like them?"

The fact that I might want to look like them didn't actually change the fact that I didn't look like them and couldn't see any way for that small miracle to occur. And my panic increased at the thought of mightily disappointing my mother when she discovered that no matter what outfit I decided to put on, I would still look like her fat, dumpy, stringy-haired daughter. In an effort to keep her hopes up, I started turning the pages more slowly, pretending to examine each photo layout, feigning interest in facial masks that came in multiple colors to match a girl's nightgown and acting as if I could actually look good in horizontal neon stripes.

Sometimes we would look at the magazine together, when I was reading an Archie comic and she came and sat by me on the couch, *Seventeen* in hand. It was by unspoken agreement that I would put the comic down and turn my attention to the glossy magazine.

"These are the new colors for fall," she said one day. "Mustard and eggplant. We'll have to get you some outfits in those colors."

Of course they would be food names, but foods that no one would want to eat, which was probably why the models were so thin. But it wasn't just the lack of any body tissue whatsoever that made them so different from me. Every head of hair, except for Twiggy's, was at least breast length, possibly to cover up the fact that the models had none, and was stick straight and shiny, as if the individual hairs had been stretched into place like taffy. Their eyes were wide, shocked, and empty. And they rarely smiled – probably because they were hungry.

It was hard not to give in, though. My mother, sitting next

to me, greasy faced and pin curled, preserving herself for the moment my father would come home from work, was so filled with hope and longing that I couldn't possibly let her down. I had to pretend that there was an outside chance that I could really do this thing, so I started taking *Seventeen* very seriously.

The more carefully I read it, the more pleased she seemed, and I began admiring the clothes out loud and even pointing out my favorites to her. The charade eventually became so second nature to me that I was actually able to get her excited about our shopping trip to the outdoor mall. And even I became optimistic – it would be a mother/daughter outing that would put me in her favor. I could pretend, for a few hours, that we really had something in common.

Going shopping at the mall had been a dismal chore for me since the time that I became unable to wear clothes off the rack. It was so much more comfortable to sit at home in front of the Sears catalog, where I wasn't confronted with slender girls heading toward the dressing rooms, arms laden with clothes, only to appear a few minutes later looking good enough to pose in front of everyone by the three-way mirror.

The fact that shopping was so enjoyable for most of the people I saw at the mall just made it that much more miserable for me. And this mall was big and sunny, stretched out over more than a city block, with new stores specifically for fashionable teenaged girls with small waists and silky hair. The only good thing about the mall was Montgomery Wards, which housed a small snack shop in the basement where doughnuts were fried fresh all day long. They would be my reward for waddling in the hot sunshine from store to store with my mother.

Seventeen wasn't wrong. Mustard and eggplant were everywhere at the mall, clinging to mannequins and dripping off racks. But the most amazing thing was that some of the clothes actually fit me. The hip-hugger skirts that had come into style hung just low enough to nestle above one roll of fat and below another. The "poor boy" sweaters were loosely constructed and stretchy, so any bulgy fat might be mistaken for casual blousiness.

I found a mustard-colored corduroy skirt to pair with a mustard-and-eggplant flowered sweater, and fishnet hose in both mustard and eggplant, so I could fool people into thinking I had two different outfits just by switching hose. But the highlight of the day, at least for my mother, was happening upon the Thermo-Jac display in one of the department stores.

I stopped dead in my tracks in the center of the "Junior" department and held out a hand to touch my mother's arm. "Mom," I said in hushed reverence, my eyes wide with wonder. "Look at that. It's the Thermo-Jac."

"Oh, my stars," she said. "That's the exact dress from *Seventeen*."

And it was. The most recent issue of *Seventeen* had run a display ad for Thermo-Jac, which was just a brand name, but seeing the featured dress right there in the store imbued the name with personal significance. The actual dress had a low-riding skirt in mustard, with a mustard-and-white-striped jersey top attached and a loose-hanging, mustard-colored plastic belt dividing the two halves.

And not only was the dress displayed prominently, but there was some kind of activity going on in the "Junior" department involving *that very dress*, the dress I recognized and was knowledgeable and fashionable enough to refer to as a Thermo-Jac. I instantly felt a part of the inner circle, that circle of models and mothers who knew what was really important in the world.

"Do you want to try it on?" my mother asked, her voice almost squeaking with anticipation.

I hesitated, terrified that it wouldn't fit. But she wanted it so desperately that I wanted it desperately, too, and I nodded.

As we got closer, I saw what the activity was – a Thermo-Jac promotion. Every girl who purchased the dress got to climb onto a makeshift platform and have her picture taken against a white backdrop for consideration in the Thermo-Jac new model search. That they would choose a fat girl with hair like a small shrub to be the next Thermo-Jac model was unlikely, but my mother had already snatched one off the rack and was heading for the dressing room.

I followed in terror. There was no way out of this. If the dress didn't fit, my mother would be crushed. If it did, I would have to pose on that platform as if I actually believed I had a chance. But my desire to continue this journey into the inner circle of beautiful women outweighed my embarrassment at having to stand on that platform while all the skinny girls who were there shopping with their mothers snickered behind their hands. All I wanted at that moment was for that dress to fit. And it did. My mother's joy was palpable, as was my relief.

"Go look at yourself," she prodded. "Go out and look in the three-way mirror."

I peeked around the curtain to make sure that no other girl was on her way out to admire herself in the same dress. Then, seeing no one, I toddled out into the open air of the store and headed for the three-way mirror. The photographer, possibly a former Thermo-Jac model herself who had aged out of the business at twenty-one, saw me and started adjusting her lens. I stared at myself from all angles, seeing the pudding-like lumps hiding just below the surface of the jersey knit.

My mother had followed me to the mirror and was admiring me from the sidelines. Her daughter could actually wear a Thermo-Jac. "Do you want it?" she asked.

I nodded. And then I was up on the platform, my heart pounding, looking around and praying that no one else in the store was watching. I didn't want anyone to think that I truly believed I could be the next Thermo-Jac model. I felt like the only one there who wasn't kidding myself.

But the photographer must have known the truth. She was only doing her job, and her job was to sell dresses. She bent me at the waist, put my left hand on my right knee, and told me to look into the distance, as if I were surveying a great ocean. The flashbulb popped and my mother beamed. As soon as it was over, I scurried back to the dressing room and the familiar comfort of my stretch pants and Snoopy sweatshirt while my mother paid for the dress. And then we went to get doughnuts.

I didn't rush home to wait for my modeling contract from Thermo-Jac to arrive in the mail. But something profound had happened that day. I had a closet full of clothes that I could actually wear, my mother seemed fond of me, and my thoughts once again began to teeter on the edge of optimism.

If I could fool my mother, a woman who saw me every day and knew what was going on under those clothes, into thinking that I was really a fashionable teenaged girl, maybe I could fool all the legitimately fashionable teenaged girls into thinking I was one of their own as well. Not since I had paraded around in my strapless gown had I felt the possibility of truly being beautiful. But now I had that Thermo-Jac, and the important values of America were once again within my grasp. And maybe – finally – the boy attacks would stop.

Queer Theory

BETWEEN ELEMENTARY SCHOOL and junior high, there is something that happens to the girls' bathroom – it starts to grow up. Like the girls who inhabit it, it is slowly taking shape and direction. An elementary school bathroom is simply a place to pee after gym class, and maybe giggle or gossip just a little, but it's simply not a social arena – not while the teacher is waiting outside for everyone to line up and walk behind her back to the classroom.

A junior high bathroom has a sense of purpose, offering a place to meet between every class so that makeup can be shared, hair can be sprayed, and absolutely up-to-the-minute, must-have news can be announced, picked apart, and reformulated into something even newer and better to take back out into the world.

For me, it was also a major seat of learning. This was where the real education took place – where I could watch the other girls and try to be like them. If I could figure that out, maybe I would stop wanting to be a boy, the girls would stop thinking I was some alien planted in their midst, and I could take my rightful place among them. I just had to take advantage of the knowledge that was offered – especially when the most popular girls were doing the teaching.

"Oooh," Melinda Banks squealed, tossing her golden curls down her back. "I looove that lipstick. Can I try it?"

"Sure. Here." Shelley Monroe handed a slim pink tube to Melinda. "It's that new one from Yardley. It'd look great on you."

I took longer than usual to wash my hands, stealing glances in the mirror at Melinda and Shelley, who were standing at the sinks next to me, trading and applying makeup, combing their hair, and generally doing what beautiful girls do in a bathroom. When I couldn't wash my hands any longer without appearing compulsive, I pulled out one paper towel and then another, drying carefully and flattering myself in my belief that Melinda and Shelley might actually notice me enough to think that I was eavesdropping.

"Who do you like in science class?" Shelley asked as she watched Melinda apply the lipstick.

"Scott Maynard," Melinda said through tightened lips. "He's cute."

"Aack, Scott Maynard," Shelley squealed. "Are you nuts? He's queer."

"Is not."

"Is so." Shelley held her palms up toward Melinda. "I swear to God he's queer. Don't you see him hanging around Bill Gibbs all the time? And he doesn't have a girlfriend. He's queer."

"You're kidding," Melinda said, giggling.

"Nuh uh. I am dead serious."

"Ewww." Melinda handed the lipstick back to Shelley and the two gathered up their books to leave.

I had pulled a third paper towel from the dispenser and was meticulously drying between my fingers. The conversation had taken a turn that caught me by surprise and intrigued me for reasons that I couldn't quite identify. As they turned and started for the door, I blurted out, "What's queer?"

Shelley and Melinda looked at each other as if the silverfish scurrying across the floor had just spoken to them. Then Shelley rolled her eyes, leaned toward me, and said, "You know. Queer. Boys who like boys."

"Ewww," Melinda said again, and the two of them disappeared through the doors, laughing at either queer boys or me.

I was late to class, but I didn't care. As I straggled through the hall, my brain was absorbing the message, turning it around and around to make sense of it. Within this bit of throwaway information that I had gleaned from Shelley Monroe was a lesson far more important than anything my teachers had to say. I knew instinctively that this had meaning for me and I just had to puzzle it out. And by the end of the day, I had.

Here was the logic: If there were truly boys who liked boys, then that must mean that those boys wanted to be girls. There was no other explanation. And if there were such boys, then they must have female counterparts – girls who wanted to be boys. And if there were girls who wanted to be boys, then those girls would have to be queer, too – which would mean that they liked girls. By virtue of this distorted reasoning, I decided that because I wanted to be a boy, I must be queer. And even though it went against every biological instinct I ever had, it meant that I had to like girls. I had no choice. It was my destiny.

While most twelve-year-old girls contemplating their own queerness in 1967 in Lincoln, Nebraska, might have been more than a little dismayed at the news, I was suddenly bordering on hysterical ecstasy. I embraced my queerness immediately. It was an answer – no, it was *the* answer. There was nothing wrong with me because I wanted to be a boy – I was just queer. That's all. The liking-girls part of the equation was momentarily overshadowed by the sheer joy of being able to name my problem. How marvelously easy everything had become.

Why this information was never brought out in health class was beyond me. Our teacher, Mrs. Ember, had never even touched on it. It was apparently far too meaningful and mysterious to be given a place in the limited junior high sex ed. curriculum. It might even be possible that none of the teachers was aware that such a state of being existed. It would be just like all of them not to know about something so monumental. But now I knew.

I woke up the next morning with an immense sense of purpose and the desire to get on with my very own queer life. *Where do I start?* I thought as I picked through my closet. *What do I do? Do I still wear these clothes or is there something else that queer girls wear? Do I still walk the same, talk the same?* I had no idea how queer girls dressed or acted or what their responsibilities were. And there probably wasn't another queer girl in the entire school, maybe not even in the entire city, who I could learn from.

I finally found my striped dress – yellow, pink, and orange, with button cuffs and a collar like a man's shirt. As I fished it out of the closet, I had another revelation – I knew what to wear and I knew what I would do. I had made a big mistake watching the girls all along, trying to figure out how to be like them, when I really should have been watching the boys.

Mary Ellen Kent's locker was right across the hall from my own. Sometimes the boys clustered there two deep, waiting for a glance, a nod, or some kind of acknowledgement from Her Highness. Mary Ellen was short, with watermelon thighs that started at the edge of her pleated skirt and morphed into blocks of calf that stopped at white bobby socks. Her nose turned up in a flip of freckles and her dark hair turned under around her jawline. She was a ninth grader, so she knew pretty much everything, and she even had the confidence to ask one of her lovesick suitors if he liked her.

I actually witnessed the scene – Mary Ellen, leaning against her locker in a seductive, fourteen-year-old pose, the white of her bobby socks peeking enticingly from her saddle shoes, the tiny black bow in her hair adding to her "come hither" persona as the question slid out of her full, freckled lips. The flustered boy probably *did* like her – it appeared that every boy did – but I didn't hear his answer, if he even gave one. I was too busy struggling to find the attractiveness in Mary Ellen.

Mary Ellen Kent is beautiful, I told myself. *Mary Ellen Kent is beautiful.* She certainly didn't measure up to any Miss America contestant I had ever seen, and those thighs would have kept her out of *Playboy* for life. But the boys obviously thought there was something to her, and now I would have to think that, too. *Mary Ellen Kent is beautiful* became my mantra. I repeated it to myself, over and over, until I was ready to believe it.

And how could I not believe it? How could she be anything but beautiful with the circus of boys who crowded her tent every day, just hoping that she would take notice? If I could figure it out, if I could be just like those boys, then I could carry out the queer life that had been predetermined for me. I knew I would soon have to make my move.

The most appropriate – in fact, the only – true means of communication in junior high outside of the bathroom was the note. It could be scribbled on the back of an old math assignment or it could be neatly handwritten on clean, lined paper, complete with little flower or heart decorations and a fancy signature with curlicues. It could be passed inside the cover of a textbook or dropped on the floor and kicked. But that was only if the recipient and the sender were in the same class. With Mary Ellen, more drastic and dangerous measures would have to be taken.

That night, I sat at my corner desk, my bedroom door closed, the hum of my parents' voices rising up from the living room. It was feverish work, but it had to be just right. I wasn't quite sure what I wanted from Mary Ellen, and I had no plan in mind beyond the moment that I would slip the note into her locker. There was some hazy, undefined thought that Mary Ellen would respond to the note, and thus to me, in a way that would put me on a par with the boys who surrounded her locker – that I would somehow become one of them simply by displaying my admiration.

That was probably how it was for queer girls, I thought, although the connection left me slightly baffled. But none of that mattered. It would all fall into place later, after Mary Ellen got the note. When I finally finished, I neatly folded the paper and slipped it into my notebook, then went downstairs to say goodnight to my parents, who were blissfully blind to the fact that their daughter had just completed a love note to a girl, something that I presumed to be the ultimate act of queerness.

The next day, I slithered out of class at the bell and slinked down the hall, taking on the role of a secret agent. I finally had a place where I fit in, and a wonderful new goal: I wasn't meant to be a beautiful woman – I was meant to pursue one. How neatly things fit into place. When I got to my locker, I fumbled with the lock, stalling for time.

Across the hall, the boys clustered and then departed, coming and going in an instant like a swarm of locusts devouring a field. When they left, Mary Ellen was gone, too, off to class, not late like I would be. I waited until the hall cleared, and then I started toward my class, swerving just slightly against Mary Ellen's locker, depositing the folded piece of paper through the slats and then moving on, as if I had merely lost my balance for a second and then recovered.

After class, I hurried back to my locker to stand idly and survey its contents while glancing over my shoulder as the note fell at Mary Ellen's feet and she let out a squeal. She quickly scooped it from the floor, clawed it open, and silently read:

Dear Mary Ellen,

I think you are beautiful. I really like you. I think you are cute and I would really like to know you better. You are really beautiful. You are the coolest girl in the school.

Your Secret Admirer

I watched as the freckles on her cheeks rose with her smile. A less-secret admirer was already standing in front of her when she looked up.

"Did you write this?" she asked the confused boy who had just happened to stumble into the middle of this romantic moment.

He should have said yes. Had he been more alert, more suave, less ninth grade and more James Bond, he could have had Mary Ellen on the spot. But he stammered and blushed and shook his head in denial, leaving Mary Ellen to question the line that was starting to form.

"Did you write this?"

She went from boy to boy, each as ignorant as the first. From my position across from Mary Ellen's court, I watched all of the jesters deny their hand in the love note. Mary Ellen was practically in a swoon when she realized that the source of this unrequited affection was not any of the usual hangers-on. It was someone quite new and different, which she must have interpreted as utterly romantic and which was exactly the reaction that I wanted her to have. Now Mary Ellen was mine, whatever that meant. It was time for my next move.

For the second night in a row, I struggled at my desk, pouring out my heart to Mary Ellen in the most eloquent language I could muster, not unlike the Renaissance poets, I was sure. By that time, I had begun to picture just what might happen when Mary Ellen read my second note. She would realize it was from me. She would look across the crowded hallway and see me there, watching her with the sullen and brooding eyes of a lover. She would know at that instant that I was the one she wanted – the man or the queer girl that I would be then, having been magically transformed by Mary Ellen's love. Finally, one of the fairy tales from my childhood would pay off. I would be transformed into a handsome princess – or prince.

I chose a different class to be late to that day, and I already had my moves down, so I easily slipped the note into Mary Ellen's locker. It said:

Dear Mary Ellen,

I think you are beautiful. I really like you. I think you are the coolest girl in the school. Maybe we could get together sometime. I hope you don't mind that I am a girl.

Your Secret Admirer

She would figure it out this time. She had to. She would look for the girl, maybe question any girls who happened to be hanging around in the hall, just like she had questioned the boys the day before. She would come up to me, displaying the note. And I would be better than those other stupid boys. I would be brighter, more alert, sophisticated and suave. I would say, "Yes, I wrote it. Of course I wrote it. Mary Ellen. My dear."

I was shamelessly visible when Mary Ellen returned to her locker after class, facing her dead on from across the hall instead of lingering at my locker and glancing over my shoulder. Shaking and struggling to calm my breath, I vowed that I would stay focused and ready for her reaction. I watched as she opened her locker and the note fell out. She squealed, just like she had the day before.

"Another note," she announced to no one, holding it in front of her and staring, appearing to savor the moment, just as I was doing from a few feet away.

Then she slowly unfolded it, this time caring for it, treating it gently like an Easter chick that she had found in a basket, nestled in pink plastic grass. By the time she had it open, her eyes were wide with wonder and her cheeks were rosy. I watched her eyes slowly scan the page as she absorbed every word. Then, in an instant, the plumpness of her cheeks disappeared into the puff of her round, freckled face, and the corners of her mouth drooped.

"Ewww," she said, and she crumpled the note and threw it down the hallway, as if just holding it were enough to contaminate her. I watched it land near a pair of white go-go boots, one toe kicking it by accident until it came to rest underneath the drinking fountain. In the meantime, Mary Ellen had slammed her locker shut and stalked down the hall, not even waiting for the boys who began to gather, confused, without her.

As I watched them, I bit my quivering lip and blinked at

the forming tears. I hadn't even had a chance. And although Mary Ellen didn't know who she had rejected, I did, and my heart was just as broken as it would have been if I had actually liked her.

My Saturday Afternoon Seduction

MY PURPLE PAINT pen was the envy of anyone who saw it. In reality, it was a tube of purple paint with a ball-point-like tip that could be used to write on walls and bulletin boards and various surfaces. My fantasy when I begged my mother to buy it was that I would artfully decorate my bulletin board with the names of the Monkees, bordered by flowers that would rival Van Gogh's irises.

What resulted was an uneven scrawl across the top of the board that said "Davy Jones." My failed artistry was disappointing at the time it happened, but the fact that there was still plenty of purple paint left in the pen made it useful as a bargaining tool. And I had a bargain to make.

Short, dark, and as round as a doughnut, Anna Trujillo did not meet any of the specifications for beauty that had been established by our founding fathers. She probably weighed less than I did, but her lack of height exaggerated the pouch of fat around her middle, just below newly formed breasts that struggled to be noticed amid her general roly-polyness. But Anna's appearance was of little concern to me. I wasn't going to marry her. I only wanted to make a trade.

"Do you want my purple paint pen?"

I had tracked Anna down in the hallway at school, and by the time I found her, I was shaking, panting, and sweat was pouring from my underarms as if some kind of dam had just broken. I would spend the rest of the day in smelly, wet misery, but if I could just get through this, it would be worth it.

Anna cocked her head, her eyes narrowing into suspicious slits. "Why?"

"Well, I just want to know if you want it. Yes or no?" *Just say yes, just say yes,* I thought. But it wasn't going to be that easy.

"You're going to give it to me?"

I sighed. "Kind of. I mean, I need you to do something for me." I glanced around the hallway as if someone might actually be paying attention to me. No one was.

"What?"

I looked around again. The halls were clearing out and we would both be late for class. I could feel the sweat behind my ears and around my collar. If I didn't say something soon, the bell would ring and she would walk away. We'd both get in trouble for nothing. I sucked in my breath then let it out along with the words.

"Iwanttomakeoutwithyouforfiveminutes."

Her eyes boggled and her face seemed to expand and redden like a ripe tomato.

"What?"

"Anna." *Please don't make me say it again.*

She shook her head and started to back away. "No. No. Are you kidding, no way, that's gross, uh uh, no chance, no deal, no –"

"Shhh," I hissed. "I'll give you my purple paint pen. I promise. Don't you want it?"

She stopped and bit her lip. I could see the gears chugging and clicking in her mind, and I relaxed a little. Finally, she said, "Okay. But just for five minutes."

"I'll time it. I promise. Just come to my house on Saturday at one."

"Okay. I gotta go," she said. Then she turned and did her

best to scurry down the hall, which was difficult on her stubby, chubby legs. But somehow she managed it, because she was gone in an instant.

I hurried away as well. Besides being late for class, it seemed that if we both got away as quickly as possible, we could pretend that the conversation had never taken place. Neither of us mentioned it for the rest of the week, but as we left school on Friday, Anna said, "See you tomorrow," and I nodded weakly. I could tell that she was already picturing how her room would look when the walls were decorated with purple flowers.

It was important for me to make out with Anna. As I sat on my bed and waited for the sound of the doorbell in the front room below, it occurred to me that there was probably something I should have done, like fixed my hair a special way or cleaned up my room. Even more important, I should have figured out exactly how this five minutes was going to go. I had one goal in mind for this experience, and that goal was a complete and total transformation.

Admittedly, this might have been an overblown expectation for a five-minute makeout session with a girl for whom I had no attraction, but I would "get to be the boy" for five minutes, which was what every queer girl wanted, and then I would instantly move into my new role with knowledge, skill, and comfort.

I looked around my bedroom. It was not exactly a venue for seduction, but the silver sparkles in the ceiling added either a sexy or a festive air. The walls were plastered with Monkees posters and my pathetic bulletin board still said "Davy Jones" in purple scrawl, but Anna had seen my room many times. She knew what to expect. I laid the purple paint pen on my dresser as further enticement for Anna, just in case my mere presence didn't light her on fire when she came in.

At the appointed hour, Anna arrived and we went upstairs to my room. My mother, who would never have allowed me upstairs with a boy, was of course not the least bit concerned about Anna. If I had truly been a lesbian, I could have had a heyday every weekend of my adolescent life, with long caucuses behind closed doors, sleepovers, and a whole array of private time alone with other girls. As it was, the next five minutes were about all I thought I'd be able to get through without fainting.

I shut the door, and Anna settled on the edge of my bed, looking slightly uncomfortable but determined. She eyed the pen as if for reinforcement. I shifted back and forth on my feet, feeling not much like the boy or the queer girl that I was hoping to morph into as soon as the scenario was underway. I finally took a deep breath, walked over, and sat beside her. How easily this had come to Toby, I thought. And then I realized that I should have prepared something, some soda that I could pour into a glass like wine or tiny snacks on a plate that I could offer.

When my voice came out of my mouth, it sounded nothing like Richard's, but that was my own fault. How could I take on Richard's role without so much as a thought to the needs of my lover? I didn't even have a smoking jacket or a bathrobe that could pass as one. I was already a flop, but there was nothing to do but forge ahead. Anna was here now, and it was not likely that I could talk her into coming back if the whole thing fell through.

"Okay," I said. "As soon as the clock hits ten after one, we'll start. Then at a quarter after, we stop. I'll watch the clock, okay?"

"Okay," she said, taking one last glance at the pen for support.

I should have told her she was beautiful. I should have taken her chin in my hand and gazed into her eyes. But we were both watching the clock, and as soon as the numbers turned over to 1:10, Anna took a deep breath, and I boldly – and clumsily – made my first move. I reached up and put my arm around her shoulders. Anna stiffened, but she gamely allowed it. Her striped knit shirt was rough against my hand, and her body did not yield passionately under my touch, as my teen romance books told me it should. But it was too late to turn back. Thirty seconds had already passed.

Now she seemed a little scared. Her eyes were wide and glassy and her lower lip quivered slightly. To avoid looking at her, I thrust my other arm in her direction and managed to grab her in an embrace. Her hair was shiny and sprayed and did not plump softly against my face as I imagined that it might. I started to peck at her shoulder through the scratchy knit and then at her neck through shellacked hair. Behind her sat the clock, and I stole a glance. One minute had passed. I either had four *whole long* minutes left or *only* four minutes left, and I wasn't sure exactly how to look at it.

It was no wonder, I thought, that girls who fooled around with boys ended up pregnant after "just one time," as Mrs. Ember had so deliberately pointed out in sex ed. There were simply no lessons on this – no instructions on courtship, no primer on romantic etiquette, no manual on proper form, no classes on what to do and how to do it.

It was a groping, grappling display of failed acrobatics, a physical free-for-all, a miserably clumsy attempt at some kind of contact and communication. I wondered if girls who were actually having "intercourse" knew that they were having it, or if they were so caught up in figuring out the motions that it only dawned on them after the baby arrived.

I knew that I was hugging Anna with far less passion than I sometimes hugged my pillow, and I loosened my grip and brought my face around to hers. I was supposed to kiss her now, and I closed my eyes and lunged at her with my face, bumping her nose with my forehead and causing her head to whip backwards as a sharp crack split the air.

"Ow," she whined, grabbing her nose.

"Oh, I'm sorry," I said, covering my mouth with my hand to keep from giggling.

As she massaged her nose, I could see the beginnings of a smile on either side of her wrist. If we weren't careful, we would both burst out in a fit of laughter, and as if we were having the same thought, we immediately straightened our mouths. Laughing would have made the whole thing funny and fun, and neither of us had ever heard Mrs. Ember say that there was any enjoyment involved in such activities. In fact, we had been taught just the opposite, so we struggled to quickly resume our composure.

"Okay," I said, holding my hands out to steady us both. "Let's start again."

"But we don't start the time over," Anna protested.

"No, no. We don't start the time over. Now let's just go."

I kept my eyes open this time and pressed my lips to hers in a firm, closed-mouth kiss. Kissing Anna was like kissing my own arm, which I had tried before with less than satisfying results. I pulled my lips away and tried again at a different angle. Nothing changed, but I could see the clock. Three minutes had passed. Why was nothing happening? Where was the jolt of electricity, the stab of emotion, the bursting inner light of self-actualization?

You're the boy, I told myself. *You're the boy. Do something.* But I didn't know what that would be, so I pulled my face away again and returned to hugging her, where I could close my eyes and pretend to be nuzzling her hair while counting down the minutes until the debacle was done. I couldn't stop now and admit to Anna and myself that we had gone through this for nothing. I had to pretend that it mattered.

When I opened my eyes again, I saw that we had fifteen seconds left. There was no panic. There was only relief. I continued to hug Anna as I silently counted the last few seconds down. Then I released her. We both let out identical involuntary sighs, but we could barely look at each other. I handed her the purple paint pen. She took it. After all, she had given me no guarantees.

"See you Monday," she said. And then she left without so much as a backward glance.

It was over.

"Oh, this is it," I said to my sparkling ceiling as I threw myself down on the bed. "You're not going to do this anymore. It's not working."

Maybe Anna's just not the right girl.

Of course she's not, she never was, but nobody else is, either.

So I'm not a queer girl after all.

Apparently not.

It wasn't long before I heard a sharp rap on the door followed by its immediate opening. My mother believed that if she knocked quickly, she could then open the door at any time of the day or night without waiting for my blessing. Then she stood at the entrance, eyeing me over her reading glasses.

"Why did Anna have your purple pen?" she asked, a solid

vertical line forming between her brows and running down like an arrow to point to the thick bridge of her glasses.

I sighed. "I traded."

"That was expensive. What did you trade for?"

"I just traded, okay? Mom, I don't feel like talking."

"Well, I don't know why we buy you things if you're going to trade them away." She closed the door and I could hear her mumbling down the hallway. "Things are expensive. Money doesn't grow on trees."

I wanted to call out to her, to say, "Mom, come back, I need to ask you something," but I didn't. There was no way that I could tell her about my failed attempt at being queer or ask her where I should go from here. I suddenly wished for my purple pen, and I stared at the empty space on my dresser where it had rested only moments before. It now seemed like a symbol of normality, and its absence was a reminder that everything had gone horribly wrong.

"Okay, I'm not queer," I said quietly to the empty room. "Then what?"

It seemed that I would have to start over again, and I wasn't sure how many times I could actually do that and maintain my sanity. But by then, I wasn't convinced that I had such a firm grip on that sanity anyway. I seemed to be just an imitation of everything that was out there to be, and I wondered if there was really anywhere to go from here. Maybe if I stayed long enough in my room, just grieving the loss of my purple pen, the world would magically change into something I could navigate. Or maybe I would magically change into someone who deserved to belong there.

Failing Sex Ed

I DON'T THINK MRS. Ember actually used the word "slut." She probably used something innocuous like "trollop" or "tramp," but the message was clear – no sex until marriage, and even then, if you enjoyed it too much, your purity could be called into question. The best thing to do was sit back and allow it, if you absolutely had to, and if you became confused, you could refer to the diagrams on the handouts that she had so carefully prepared and passed out to all the girls in her seventh grade "health" class.

And if that wasn't enough, there was another thing to worry about as well – being a "tease." Thanks to Mrs. Ember, we discovered that boys were little more than sexual bottle rockets, primed to shoot off into space if we so much as moved a hip. Of course, being a tease was far more desirable than being slut, but our concern made for several years of marching through the halls of school like stiff wooden soldiers.

None of this information made us want to have sex, putting to rest the fear that some of our parents had that learning about certain parts of the body would actually encourage their use. It wasn't the things we learned that got us into trouble, but the things we didn't learn – about dating, courtship, love, sexual orientation, mutual respect, emotions, relating to each other as people, and the fact that there was actual fun and pleasure to be had in having sex with someone else. Those things, along with 90 percent of the stuff that we forgot from sex ed. class, were what we had to learn on the street.

By ninth grade, my best friend Josie and I had perfected a skill known as "hanging out." It did not involve making troll doll clothes from tiny patterns or giving human names to ceramic animals, then walking them around the bedroom floor and making up different voices for them, activities that had seemed to hold our interest for hours when we were younger.

Hanging out consisted of loitering all day in parks, on choice streets, and in fast-food parking lots. It involved long walks to drug stores on the other side of town to procure candy necklaces, flavored lip gloss, and plastic rings. It was crucial to find a new and different place to hang out every day, and Josie and I walked for miles to find just the right Dairy Queen parking lot or busy street corner. One of the benefits of all that walking was that it caused me to drop a lot of weight without trying. Another was that we met people who could teach us things. In my case, one of those things was how to be the right kind of girl.

By the time we discovered Barb Leonard and DeDe Granger, Josie and I were skilled hanger-outers. The problem was that we were still walking around stiff-hipped from Mrs. Ember's warnings, and although we often ventured to the outskirts of town, we were still trapped within the limits of our own pathetic sexual knowledge.

We were almost in high school and neither one of us had ever kissed a boy, which we considered a prerequisite for entering the tenth grade. Sex and love, in very general terms, were topics of our everyday conversation, but the details were hazy. We knew that it really wasn't good to be a "slut." We knew we were supposed to wait until marriage, but that seemed like a long way off, and at the rate that we were being asked to go steady, marriage was probably out of the question anyway. Josie gamely insisted that she was going to wait, but I wasn't so sure. If sex with a girl wasn't the answer to my problem, then maybe sex with a boy was. We both wanted to know more. And that's where Barb and DeDe came in.

Josie and I met them on one of our many forays into the city in search of places to hang out. They were sitting in a King's fast-food restaurant miles from our own neighborhood, looking like seasoned veterans of the hanging-out game. They were so appealing, with their strawlike bleached-blonde hair and their matching black-ringed eyes and hot-pink cheeks, that we chose to sit in the booth right next to theirs, even though every other booth and table in the place was empty. And when we sat down, they actually spoke to us.

"Look at all my rings," Barb said as we wiggled into our seats, shoving her hand across the top of the booth to reveal a variety of cheap gold and silver bands on every finger.

"Wow," I said, more impressed by the fact that a cool girl had actually spoken to me than I was by the rings. "Where'd you get them all?"

"Boys," DeDe piped up. "She's going with a boy from every school. None of them knows about the other ones, though."

"Yeah," said Barb. "When I'm with one, I just take all the other rings off. But sometimes I forget which one gave me which, so then I get in trouble."

"But not for long," DeDe said. "She can make them forget that they're mad."

Then they both screeched and giggled at a wonderful private joke that I didn't understand.

"How do you do that?" I asked, which made them screech and giggle again.

When they finally regained their composure, Barb grinned and said, "You know. Sixty-nine."

I glanced at Josie, who shrugged.

"Six-D-Nine?" I said, turning back to Barb.

"Sixty-nine. Sixty-nine," DeDe squealed, and then they both burst into another fit of giggles.

When they stopped laughing, Barb looked at me for a second and her expression turned to one of serious concern. "You know," she said, nodding her head in encouragement. "Sixty-nine."

I must have looked blank and stupid, because her whole presentation morphed into that of Mrs. Ember, as if she were explaining something very scientific.

"You put his peter in your mouth and he puts your pussy in his."

Now Mrs. Ember never would have used those terms, but I knew what peter and pussy meant from lessons I had learned in the girls' bathroom at school. I just didn't know that there were such creative things that could be done with them. And I honestly didn't want to know that this was the only way I could collect rings from boys. Barb and DeDe seemed to sense my apprehension and recognize their superiority. Instantly, DeDe pulled her shirt collar aside.

"And look at this," she said proudly.

Josie gasped and scrunched up her face. "Ewww, what is it?"

We both stared at the huge red bruise that DeDe was displaying. It took up half of one side of her neck and splayed out into uneven edges, as if a dodge ball had smacked her there from just a few feet away.

"It's a hickey," she said. "My boyfriend gave it to me. See, it's in the shape of a heart with an arrow through it."

If I squinted hard enough and pretended a lot, I could almost see the heart and the arrow. But the shape of the thing wasn't important. The fact was that I also knew what a hickey was, even though this was the first time I had ever seen one, and I instantly wanted one of my own. Even more, I wanted a boyfriend who would give me one and several boyfriends who would give me rings. Neither Josie nor I had anything on our body that we could show to these girls that would mark us as their equals. And, soon enough, they got bored showing off and left. As they walked out, I noticed two scoops of butt cheek hanging from below the hem of Barb's shorts.

After that encounter, I paid more attention than ever to sex. I listened even more carefully in the bathroom. I didn't miss a thing when Kristi Evans, the new girl in our class, announced loudly upon her arrival, "Fingering is my hobby. I used to do it with all the boys at my old school." I also knew what that was, and I saw that her outspoken support of it resulted in her going steady with the most popular boy in class by the end of the day.

Waiting until marriage wasn't going to cut it when there were girls like Barb and DeDe and Kristi Evans around. Waiting until marriage was a fool's game. The coolest and most popular girls weren't waiting, and the fact that Mrs. Ember was neither cool nor popular made her admonishments all that much more unimpressive. I needed to find out about sex now. I needed to know if it would make things right – if it would transform me into the girl I was supposed to be. I felt that I had already waited too long. I just had to find someone to have sex *with*.

When I learned about Elliott Mahoney, I decided that he would be the one. He sniffed airplane glue, opposed the Vietnam war, and was a social outcast, which made it less likely that girls offered up their body to him on a regular basis, and more likely that he would accept mine. I had never seen him, but even that fact imbued him with a certain glamour that other boys, who were known entities, were lacking. I was already in love with Elliott Mahoney. He would have to have four legs and a tail for me not to proceed with my plan. Somehow, I had to convince Elliott to have sex with me. It was surprisingly easy, actually – all I had to do was ask.

For our sexual tryst, Elliott and I met in the middle of a thicket of trees in College View Park, far away from the picnic tables and playground equipment that invited families for weekend outings. It was a sturdy, entangled cluster of trees, protected on all sides by bushy pines spreading out from a nucleus of twiggy and spindly adolescent saplings. Although the park took up only one city block, with houses across the street in all directions, no one could hear us at 10:30 on a Saturday morning.

Our only preparation had been to work out the terms, which involved Elliott arriving at College View Park with a blanket and a condom, and me just arriving. The condom part was one of the few valuable things that I had learned – and remembered – from sex ed.

"How about right here?" Elliott said after we made our way through the scratchy bushes and trees that composed the thicket. He held out his crumpled red blanket like a matador trying to entice a bull. The blanket was worn, its fibers stretched thin with use, and it was scratched and matted, as if he had pulled it from the floor of a doghouse. But we had gone this far, and I certainly would not have been allowed to leave the house unquestioned with a blanket under my arm, so I had to take what I could get.

"Okay," I said, nodding.

The mosquitoes had already started to buzz around my

head, and I could hear a strange buzzing inside my ears as well. I wasn't quite sure what I was supposed to be doing. The only thing I could remember from my lessons on the street was that a man got on top of a woman, put his penis into her "hole," and then, when everything started to foam like a washing machine, it was over.

Elliott had the blanket spread out over a pebbly and pine-needley patch of dirt, and he kneeled down, as if getting ready to pray toward Mecca.

"Take off your pants and lay down," he insisted.

He was obviously taking charge, which gave me hope that he might know what to do, so I unzipped my jeans and wiggled out of them. I was instantly embarrassed by my white cotton Carters, a comfortable holdover from my younger days, and I dropped to a cross-legged sitting position and let the tails of my shirt hang over them. The ground was hard beneath the thin, nappy blanket. Pine needles poked my butt, and mosquitoes flitted around my pale, exposed legs.

Elliott sat down, too, with his back to me, and pulled out his condom. He got it open with relative ease, but then he started to struggle mightily. All I could see were his arms moving and the clench of his jaw. Finally, I leaned forward and peeked over his shoulder.

I wasn't exactly sure what a teenaged boy's penis was supposed to look like, but I remembered Mrs. Ember saying something about "engorged with blood," which suggested the unpleasant visual of a Rocky Mountain tick. I preferred my friend Anna's explanation on one of our sleepovers – that when a boy got "turned on," his penis got "hard." She had a lot of little brothers and somehow ought to know. How hard it was supposed to get, I didn't know, but Elliott's penis resembled a lump of taffy after a few good pulls – soft and spindly and white.

To pass the time, I unbuttoned my shirt. I figured it would have to come off eventually, along with my bra. When I slid these barriers off my body and onto the dirt next to the blanket, Elliott turned his head and looked at me. Whatever I had done, it worked, because within a few seconds, Elliott turned his lower half around to reveal a secured condom on what I guessed was a hard penis.

"Are you ready?" he asked.

His penis jerked rigidly to one side, then the other. It seemed slightly unanchored and unsure of itself. But I nodded and scooted myself into a supine position on the blanket, slipping out of my white cotton Carters. At that point, I was not so much afraid as I was painfully hot and uncomfortable in the middle of the airless grove, and I wondered why people actually did this thing when they didn't absolutely have to.

My makeup felt thick and heavy on my face, and my pores seemed to be gasping for air. My scalp was starting to sweat, along with my back and the backs of my legs, pressed firmly against the hot red blanket. The sweat seemed to be a signal to the mosquitoes, who began to nibble here and there. I wiggled to make them go away, but Elliott apparently took it as a sign, and practically threw his body on top of mine.

Then I felt the penis between my legs. Elliott was gamely making thrusting motions with his hips, stabbing his "peter" in the vicinity of my "pussy." We both knew there was an entry point somewhere, but neither of us was sure how to get there. Suddenly Elliott seemed as clueless as I was. I had never taken the time to examine my genitals and paid little attention in health class when they were being described, so I wasn't quite sure exactly where his point of entry might lie. But I was going to endure this endless, repetitive poking, because there was no way that I was going to suggest giving up and reverting to the fallback position of "Six-D-Nine." Finally, after several more jabs, something seemed to give way. I let out a little grunt as I felt my body being penetrated. Then Elliott began to pump.

The movement actually seemed to encourage, rather than frighten, the mosquitoes, who advanced on us like warships. The blanket collected loose pine needles with each movement of Elliott's body, and they all found their way underneath my bare rear end.

For my own part, I stayed rigid and still, fearing that any motion might cause Elliott's penis to come loose. If that happened, we might never find the opening again. Elliott looked like a man possessed, his face set in grim determination, as if completing this act were the most important, and the most difficult, thing that he would ever do in his life. His glasses fell off. He ignored this and continued, brave in the face of sightlessness. My jaw was tightly clenched, although I only realized it later, when a dull ache reminded me as I chewed my dinner. I was certain that I was supposed to be doing something, anything, to help Elliott, since he looked so overburdened with the effort. I wondered when the foaming would start and how I would know.

And then, something happened. Elliott stopped and, for a second, hovered above me, oblivious. His face contorted, as if a wasp had just stung his bare behind. For a moment, I was afraid. If he passed out or if he died out there, what would happen? How could I explain this to my parents, and what could I possibly say to Elliott's mom? This would be trouble for sure. But then his face smoothed, and he pulled himself away from me, grabbed his penis, and raised his body to bring the organ within my line of vision.

"Do you want some more?" he asked, suddenly leering,

instantly transformed into a slimy lounge singer – or a boy who had just lost his virginity.

I looked at the penis. The condom was still in place, its tip filled to bursting with gooey liquid. I didn't want more, but I thought that I might hurt his feelings if I said no, so I nodded. Elliott was still grinning like a lecher as he attempted reentry. To my relief, and possibly to his, it didn't work. His penis had turned droopy and uncooperative. We were done.

There was no shame for me in the aftermath of this experiment. Even though Elliott and I were completely naked and were fumbling through the underbrush to retrieve our clothes, there was something acceptable about what had just happened. Mrs. Ember wouldn't think so, but everything I'd learned outside of sex ed. class told me that this was normal. We were supposed to be doing this, at least in a general sense. But I wasn't impressed. I finally understood why Josie said she was going to wait until marriage before "doing anything." Who wouldn't want to wait as long as possible before going through something like that?

But I was still mired in expectation. If I did it, I was a slut. If I didn't do it, I was a tease. Elliott was swollen like a puffer fish over his conquest, and I was still trying to figure out which label I wanted to live with. So far, neither of them had been exactly right. What label would Elliott get for his efforts? From the way he looked, I suspected that it would be something far grander than even Mrs. Ember could imagine.

Regardless, I had learned something pretty important – as uncomfortable as it was, I was meant for the bumbling, stumbling interaction that I had suffered through with Elliott. I was meant not to give rings, but to get them. I was meant to be lured into bedrooms, not to lure someone else there.

No matter how I felt inside, no matter what questions or

confusions or convoluted thinking I had, I was a girl. I was a girl who liked boys. And the only thing I could do about it was become the best girl – and later, the best woman – I could possibly be.

With the limited options available to me, that's exactly what I did – and, for quite a while, it worked.

A Short Womanhood

MY "WOMANHOOD" LASTED from the time I lost my virginity until my early forties, when I first discovered that there was a more technical name than "boy attacks" for what I was feeling, that I wasn't the only one, and that there were more successful remedies than making out with Anna Trujillo, writing love notes to Mary Ellen Kent, or even having sex with Elliott Mahoney.

There are many things that I did as a female of which I'm very proud. I was a caseworker, a teacher, and a volunteer for various causes. I helped a lot of people, and I even saved some lives. But underlying – or overshadowing – it all was my attempt to be the "best woman I could be," based on the standards of beauty and womanliness that I had bought into many years before. An ex and I used to joke that the writing on my tombstone would be "How does my hair look?"

If I had to sum up my womanhood in one word, it would probably be "makeup." And if I had to sum it up in one essay, it might the following one.

Beauty's Only Skin Deep, but Shallow Goes All the Way to the Bone

THERE ARE TWO kinds of beautiful people in the world – those who wake up beautiful and those who wake up early. When you aren't beautiful by nature, but when everything around you tells you that you should be, you learn to get by on very little sleep.

My beauty was there, but it took awhile to assemble it – about an hour and a half every morning. I figured out once that, by age forty, I had spent three and a half years of my life just getting ready.

It's all gone now, but sometimes I miss all the fuss and pageantry. I probably kept the entire beauty industry solvent for over three decades. And I never even received a thank you – just a free gift with purchase.

Learning to be beautiful was quite a process, but once I had it figured out, it became an obsession, a constant working and reworking of what was there and what wasn't, a full awareness at all times of what I had and what I lacked. It became a lifestyle that began when I forced myself out of bed before the rest of the world had even entered REM sleep and ended when I finally took it all off, with just as many astringents and lotions and creams as I had used to put it on in the first place – if I had the energy left to do so. As I grew into adulthood, I learned even more tricks and techniques, and the tools that I needed became far more expensive and extensive than just a handful of drugstore cosmetics.

If I lived with a man, I had to get up even earlier, long

before he did, so that I would be "ready" – complete and whole – by the time he awoke. I would be the beautiful woman that he remembered going to sleep with, since I only took my makeup off after the lights were out and he was already safely in bed.

It didn't help that one of my boyfriends told me that he never would have asked me out if he had seen me first without makeup. It also didn't help that my role model in life was a mother who had gotten up at midnight to apply her makeup on three consecutive nights when she thought she was in labor. She wanted to look good when she got to the hospital to give birth, because creating another human being, mostly by herself, was apparently not enough.

When I lived alone, there was still cause for concern. That cute guy next door might actually choose an inopportune, makeupless time to look through his window into mine or to come over to borrow some sugar for a cake that he suddenly got the urge to bake right after I had washed my face or right before I had put my face on. And of course, he could be The One, my Prince Charming, my Happily Ever After, the guy that I was supposed to have built my life around waiting for – and I would have blown it. He would have seen me for what I really was – even if I wasn't sure myself.

It wasn't going to happen to me. Everything in my history told me that it didn't have to. I had the power to fix it. I knew all the tricks. I would take care of it, just as I had been taught to do.

My ritual was exhausting. Up at 5:30 every morning for a shower that always included a shave – both legs and underarms, every day, winter or summer, no stubble allowed. Pink Daisy razors decorated every surface that lay behind the shower curtain. After my shower, which often included rubbing a gritty exfoliating scrub on my limbs to get rid of any layer protecting the pink, raw skin underneath, came the lotion – and not just any lotion. It had to smell like something – preferably exotic flowers, coconuts, or vanilla. But that was the easy part. Next came the face.

There was moisturizer, then foundation, highlighter under the brows, contour in the crease of the eye, shadow on the lid, eyeliner, eyelash curler, mascara, eyebrow pencil, blush for contour, blush for color, powder to set it all, lipliner and lipstick. After that came the forty-five-minute blow dry, each section of hair wrapped over a monster round brush and pulled tight, then rewound, then pulled tight, then rewound, until I looked like a TV anchorwoman. Then it had to be teased at the roots and shellacked with hair spray until it could stand alone and live a perfectly normal life by itself in the event that I checked out unexpectedly. Perfume was the finishing touch, enough to announce that I was entering a room, enough to deny that I had ever left it.

Of course, I was still naked. The body needed clothes, and I had a closet full – slinky dresses of floral-patterned silk, long, full skirts in colorful prints, four or five pairs of identical black Capri pants, and four or five identical tight black T-shirts that clung to my pushed-up breasts. And shoes – from practical pumps with one-inch heels to exotic, tottering four-inch-heeled boots and sandals. Silver bangle bracelets that ran halfway up both forearms, huge gold hooped earrings or long, dangly ones, rope necklaces, bead necklaces, chains, sometimes even an oversized gold pin with stars hanging down in a sparkly column.

When I was finished, I looked like a Christmas tree without the lights, and I still hadn't covered enough. It still might be possible for someone to look so close that they would see what was underneath – whatever that was.

It was hard to move. The stiffness of my hair signaled to the rest of my body that stiffness was required, that any sudden movement might start an unraveling of the whole process that would leave me puddled on the floor like the Wicked Witch of the West. Beauty had won out there, too. If I laughed too hard, tears formed in my eyes, threatening to smear the carefully applied eyeliner and mascara. If I walked too fast, if I jogged, if I danced – well, sweat is a natural enemy of makeup. In the wild, the two are known to form a predator/prey relationship.

And I'm pretty sure that there's a chemical in sweat that eats away at even the most viscous of hair products, reducing a carefully constructed style to a limp and soggy mass of random strands, much like an old-fashioned kitchen mop. So sweating was simply not allowed. I took up tennis once and sweat so much that my eyes burned and swelled with the mascara that ran into them and then down my face in rivulets of mud. I didn't stop wearing makeup to the tennis court – I stopped playing tennis. Violent movement of any kind was simply out of the question.

It was also difficult to move with any meaning with a ten-pound purse attached to my shoulder like a newborn infant in a sling. My purse itself didn't actually weigh ten pounds, but it had to be big enough to hold ten pounds of stuff. Ten pounds of stuff consisted of two full makeup bags, dental floss, a toothbrush and paste, a small hair pick, a large hair pick, a hairbrush, a compact, nail polish to repair chips, nail polish to repair runs in hose, emery boards, a travel-sized hairspray, a full-sized spray bottle of eau du toilette, breath mints, Kleenex, and a handful of lipsticks. Oh, there was a billfold in there, too, but it never had any money in it. All the money was in the bank accounts of the cosmetic company

CEOs. I leaned to one side like the Tower of Pisa, and I might have permanently damaged my posture, but there was no sacrifice to great for the cause.

Silver bangle bracelets also have a tendency to impair movement, especially when they run up an entire arm and clink and clang like Jacob Marley's ghost. The bracelets were so raucous at one professional meeting that I tried to slip them off unobtrusively, at which time they rebelled and went scattering across the floor like loose marbles, clinking and clanging all the way. The others pretended not to notice, which is why they were called professionals.

High heels echo on linoleum or hardwood floors. I had to walk slowly so as not to constantly announce my arrival. Long nails have a tendency to break during any purposeful activity. I once taped every finger with masking tape so my nails would survive a volleyball game. It was unattractive and difficult to undo. I quit playing volleyball. Pantyhose snag and the wires in push-up bras eventually push through. The solution to it all was not to move. It made it hard to go anywhere, but I didn't want to go anywhere if I didn't look just right. What was the point of going out if I risked discovery – if people might see the dark underbelly of my attractiveness?

Had I not been transgender, I would have continued to survive on very little sleep, and I would have eventually aged out of the chosen group anyway. But instead, I relinquished my rights to the privilege of beauty voluntarily, and I try not to look back.

Do I miss it? Sure I do – sometimes. My appearance was the one marker I had that let me know that everything was okay – at least with me – and that if something wasn't okay, it could be fixed. And I miss it when I walk into a jewelry store and see the perfect pair of earrings, or when one of my female friends shows up in an outfit that would have looked great on me. I miss it when I remember some of the privilege it afforded me in my everyday life, the special treatment I got from both men and women because I possessed something of value in a culture that treasures it.

But mostly I don't miss it, because the expectations and responsibilities that went with it were too much of a burden to bear, and having it, if even part-time, gave me a pretty skewed impression of the world.

I was only able to realize it in hindsight, when it was all taken away, and even then, the transition was gradual. I had originally hoped to resemble Brad Pitt, but when I finally came to terms with the fact that I turned out more like Wilford Brimley, I was able to take a guilty pleasure in just being comfortable for a change. At least I got to move a little, and I quit worrying about whether or not I was the best-looking one in any room – I wasn't. I never am. But I have a little more time, a little more money, and a lot more self-confidence than I did before.

To what extent my obsession was fueled by gender identity issues, I will never know. Appearance and I go way back. And although transition resulted in a "way out" of the trap, it wasn't intended to be. I didn't realize until it was all over that there was any "out" to be had, because I truly wasn't aware that I was "in" anything. The never-ending beauty spiral of my female life only became apparent to me when I was no longer spinning in its center.

Even then, it took some time to finally see my value as a whole human being – a plain, simple, nondescript, everyday whole human being who is actually able to move now, because the weight of my purse – and the world – is off my shoulders.

A Short Manhood
(in more ways than one)

THERE ARE TIMES when I feel as if my decision to transition was very abrupt, and there are other times when I realize that my entire life was "symptomatic" of the day when this would come. It might have happened much earlier if I'd had the Internet and a smart phone instead of the Dewey Decimal System and the junior high library.

But it might not have. It's hard to know what would have happened, or how my life might have turned out, if I hadn't gone to a therapist for an unrelated issue, if I hadn't casually shared my "secret" with a slip of the tongue, and if my therapist hadn't taken me seriously and insisted that I tell her what I meant when I said, "I've always wanted to be a guy."

I didn't intentionally go to a "gender therapist." What I did was go to the only therapist in my HMO who happened to have an opening at the time. That she turned out to be a specialist in gender issues who knew enough to look beyond the big hair, makeup, high heels, and floral-print dress and recognize the significance of what I saw as a throwaway comment is almost beyond coincidence.

But as just about any trans person can attest, once the "condition" is identified and the solution becomes apparent, a type of snowball effect takes place, and you are rolling down the hill, collecting not only snow, but all the scattered pieces of yourself as well. What follows are some of the attempts to put those pieces together into some coherent life form – a trans guy.

In the Beginning . . .

I HAD DRIVEN around for two hours – up and down the street, around the block, down a side street, then another, then back. Every time I drove by the building, I looked, I studied, but there were no signs of life, no signs that anything might be going on there at all. It was already dark, but the mirrored front kept me from seeing any lights on inside.

There was a trailer court across the street, mobile homes scrunched together in perfect rows like kernels on a corn cob, a few porch lights on, but curtains drawn – they were in for the night.

But maybe, just maybe, someone was looking out. Maybe they were all looking out, staring over at the gravel parking lot on the other side of the street, waiting to see who pulled in. And I was absolutely certain that they would all know why I was there. They would take down my license plate number, call it in, find out who I was, and I would see it in the headlines the next day.

I could feel my heart beating in my chest, in my neck, in my stomach – a full-body metronome that let me know how scared I was just in case I happened to forget. But I didn't forget. Every time I drove past the place, my heart lurched, stopped, then started up again. There's no meeting here, I thought. There's nobody here. I need to go home.

But there was a meeting there, and I knew that. My therapist said I was ready, that I needed to go. But what if someone saw me? There was an invisible safety barrier, right at the edge of the street, right where the gravel parking lot began, and once I crossed that, sirens would blare, a giant spotlight would come on and engulf the car in brilliance, balloons would be released, and all the trailer watchers would come out. Maybe a news van would pull up and a stiff-haired reporter would jump out and shove a microphone toward the car.

"We know who you are. We know why you're here. Care to comment?"

But it was almost time for the meeting to start. I had to go or drive away. And as I passed the building one more time, I held my breath and jerked the steering wheel to the right. My tires hit gravel and I was in the parking lot. I was across the barrier. And nothing happened. I had to sit there for a few minutes, simply to acknowledge that I had made it that far without detection. But I still had to get out of the car. And then what would happen?

I was finally able to open the car door and scurry into the building as if a sudden downpour had taken me by surprise, and once I was inside, I was in even more of a hurry. Because this was an office building, and even though it appeared deserted, the offices closed for the night, someone still might see me – a janitor maybe, or someone working late. I just had to find the place, get to that one certain door.

I clambered up the steps and down the hall, searching, the office doors all looking a little tentative, as if one of them might open at any minute. But none of them did, and soon I was in front of the door that said "The Gender Identity Center of Colorado," and I couldn't decide whether it was scarier now to be in the hall or to go inside.

I was trapped. I could feel my heart again, and I could feel the sweat under my arms and down my back. The sign on the door said "Shove Hard," and so I did, stumbling into the room. And there I stood, a sense of numb panic mingling with relief that I had actually managed to get there at all.

The room looked like someone's small home – threadbare carpeting with what used to be some kind of green and maroon pattern, pale green walls, and, against a far wall, mismatched couches surrounding a weathered coffee table.

Trans people don't have a lot of money, as I would find out later when I officially became one, and neither do their organizations. Gender centers are usually funded through donations, membership fees, and door fees from meetings. Most of the members save every penny with an eye to expensive hormone treatments and surgeries that insurance doesn't pay for. So whatever space is affordable, whatever items are donated – that's what makes up a center.

And it was, in fact, a center, an organization, rather than just a meeting place. On my left, a glass counter displayed some books and pins and rainbow knickknacks along with gaudy costume jewelry and size-16 pumps. Behind it, a row of mailboxes held correspondence for the volunteer officers. On the opposite wall, two banners proclaimed again that this was "The Gender Identity Center of Colorado," as if the plus-sized pumps hadn't given it away. I was in the right place. But there was no one there.

"Hello?" I squeaked out, and I heard a shuffling around the corner. In a minute, someone appeared. We both stared, sizing each other up as if we had met face to face in a dark alley after midnight.

I didn't know who or what this person was. Much shorter than me, with a rounded face that looked almost prepubescent and hair the length of whisker stubble, this could have been a twelve-year-old boy. There was also the remote possibility that this was somehow a girl – a girl with a hormone imbalance, a girl who really wasn't a girl at all.

But this was not the kind of girl I was familiar with, not the kind that I spent my life attempting to become. If this was a girl, I could have shown her how to lose that hair on her upper lip. But then I remembered that I was here to see Jonathan, and the thing that finally made the most sense was that this was him.

"Are you ... Jonathan?" My voice shook. I cleared my throat.

"Uh huh," the person said, still studying me.

"I'm ... Jennifer?" I put my hand out and saw that it was shaking as much as my voice. "I, uh, I ... e-mailed? About the group?"

"Oh, yeah." He took my hand and pumped it as if we were old friends, but he still looked wary. And I understood why.

What he saw was a woman, 5'7", 145 pounds, with shoulder-length, golden-red hair that had been carefully blown dry over a giant round brush. He saw a woman with three shades of eye shadow, artfully blended to create a highlight below the brow, shading in the crease, and a splash of brightness on the lid.

This woman, with sizable breasts made fuller by a Frederick's of Hollywood push-up bra and a thin waist captured by a wide black belt decorated in gold, was clutching her leather shoulder bag and shuffling back and forth in her spike-heeled black boots in the lobby of The Gender Identity Center of Colorado. She was there for the female-to-male support group. Jonathan was her first trans man. And she might very well be his first ultra-femme transgender FTM. He looked unconvinced.

"Um, come on in," he said, jerking his head toward the couches in the back of the room. "Sit down."

"My therapist told me to come," I said, feeling the need to apologize for being so blatantly a woman. I perched on the edge of the couch with my purse in my lap and my knees pulled together, while Jonathan plopped into an easy chair opposite me, slinging one leg over the side. I glanced around the room, avoiding what had now become Jonathan's slightly amused and casual gaze. "I, um, have ... gender issues."

He nodded and ran a hand across the stubble on his head. I was sure he could see that I had gender issues – it was only a matter of which gender I had an issue with. My big hair and full makeup might have suggested that I would soon be admiring the costume jewelry and XXL shoes. But Jonathan was up in a flash and into the other room, returning with a book that he laid out on the coffee table.

"You might want to look at this," he said. "You should really buy this. I recommend it to all the guys. It might help you decide what you want to do."

But as I reached for the book, Loren Cameron's *Body Alchemy: Transsexual Portraits*, someone else shoved hard and burst through the door – someone who actually belonged there, someone with short, spiky hair, men's shorts, hairy legs, and breasts bound tightly with an ACE bandage. Someone named Kelly, I would soon find out, and Kelly was having a bad day.

I put the book down and tried to make myself invisible. I was a fraud next to Kelly, who was so obviously trans, so obviously male. It seemed almost an insult to Kelly that I was sitting there, pretending to be just like him.

"I'm still getting ma'amed all the time," Kelly moaned. "Every day it gets harder and harder for me when I'm seen as a female. I just can't stand it anymore."

Kelly was talking to Jonathan, not to me, which was

understandable. One look at me made it obvious that there was no way I could relate to this problem. Everyone I came in contact with saw me as a female – there's just no mistaking flawlessly applied lipliner. So Jonathan and Kelly talked and I listened.

I listened to the pain of being seen as female when one knows himself to be male. I listened to the agony of not being able to get hormone shots yet, of having to wait for the therapist to approve them with her letter. No doctor would give hormone shots without a therapist's letter. What if the person changed his mind? But I knew from looking at Kelly that he would never change his mind. And I knew from looking at Jonathan, who had already been on hormones for almost a year, that he would never change his mind. Was I like them? That was what I was there to find out. But I already knew the answer.

I wasn't like them – not in the way I dressed, or walked, or talked, or acted. But, in an even more important way, I *was* like them or I wouldn't be there at all. We were transgender, all of us. We had been born with a "female" body, but we were really male. Would I ever be where Kelly was, I wondered, with short hair and bound breasts, agonizing over the world's natural misconception about my gender? It seemed impossible. If being male was home for me, I was on the other side of the world.

"I'm not sure what to do," I finally blurted out. "I mean, I'd have to get a nose job. My nose is too small."

My nose is too small. It was the one thing that I would worry about. Maybe I could get out of the whole thing simply by acknowledging that my nose was too small to ever be a man's nose, that the solution to this problem was simply not going to fit me.

Maybe Jonathan would say, "Yeah, you're right. It's probably not going to work for you." Maybe Kelly would say, "Nose surgery is so expensive. Might as well forget all of it." Or maybe they would just laugh. But they didn't say those things and they didn't laugh. Apparently every concern was legitimate here.

"Don't change your nose," Jonathan said, with a fervor indicating that he thought I was on my way to the plastic surgeon right after the meeting. "Your face will change."

"Yeah," Kelly said, nodding. "Testosterone changes your face. Wait and see what you look like first. You have no idea how your face will look in a year."

They had taken me seriously. Even in my high-heeled boots, even with the scent of my perfume still hanging in the air, they believed that I was one of them. Underneath everything, they saw it, and I felt vindicated and terrified. I wanted to leave and I wanted to stay, but it didn't matter. The meeting was over. It was time for the five-dollar fee. I had a ten and Jonathan had no change. But Kelly had five ones.

"Well," Jonathan said to Kelly, "you give your five ones to him ..." He nodded his head toward me. "And he can give me his ten."

It took me a minute to realize that he was talking about me. Him. Give your five ones to him. It was ludicrous and I tipped my head down so that my hair hung in my face. I could feel my cheeks redden at the ridiculousness of the pronoun at the same time that the corners of my mouth turned upward against my will.

This was the language of the FTM meetings. And I was "him" there, no matter what I looked like. How could it be so? When I got home, I looked in the mirror and there wasn't a trace of "him" to be found.

You're kidding yourself, I thought as I leaned closer to examine the makeup that had made it through the day and was still appropriately in place. You're not like them. This isn't going to happen to you.

But the next day, I was at the bookstore ...

I had a mission, just like the night before, and as soon as I walked in the door, I was sure that everyone in the store, from the gray-haired lady flipping through cookbooks to the clerk with six piercings in the top half of his face, knew why I was there.

At first, I pretended to browse. I glanced idly at books that were of no interest, suddenly fascinated by antique cars and Southwestern decorating schemes. I was inching my way to the gay and lesbian section of the store, ever conscious that the back of my blouse was darkening from sweat and that I looked so suspicious that the clerks were probably eyeing my oversized purse.

As I reached my target, I froze. *They'll think I'm a lesbian. That is, if they don't figure things out right away.* My hair was perfect, my makeup flawless, my heels high. I was so stiff and prissy that even lesbians wouldn't want to claim me, but that made no difference. I was pretty sure that everyone was looking, making their assessments, rendering their judgments.

I tried to look confused, as if I had stumbled on the queer books by mistake and was too baffled by them to move on. And then I saw it – one small shelf above the gay men's erotica, one short stretch of books labeled "gender studies." I looked around and saw that everyone had apparently turned away from me for just a moment, so I had a burst of time to frantically study the titles. But it wasn't there. I read each title, each author, I glanced around, I turned back – it wasn't there.

But I knew they had it somewhere. Which meant that I either had to leave without my purchase – or I had to ask.

There was a line at the checkout counter. I walked up and patiently waited my turn, glancing behind me to see who might overhear my question to the clerk. When I got to the front of the line, I leaned forward, as if I were going to tell the clerk a monumental secret – and in a way, I felt that I was. I thought he might take my body language and my lowered voice as clues on how to conduct his own responses, but I was wrong.

"I'm looking for a book," I said, my voice and my chin dropping.

"What?" He was young, the one with all the piercings, and he was using his reserved-for-old-ladies voice. I was, after all, probably twenty years his senior.

"A book," I said, raising my head a little.

"Well, they're divided by subject. What's it about?" His voice was so loud that he could have been talking to the person at the back of the line, who was quite a distance away now. I turned my head to see that several people were shifting impatiently behind me.

"Um. Transsexuals."

"What?"

"Transsexuals," I said more forcefully, my perspiration level rising with my voice.

"Gender section," he called out to the entire floor of customers. "With the *gay* and *lesbian*."

"It's not there."

"Oh, well, go ask that lady over there."

He motioned to a desk with a computer, and I edged my way by the people in line, ignoring the glares of disgust that were obviously due to my gender flaw. As I approached the woman at the computer, I decided to pretend that I was a sociologist or a psychologist or a professor. I wanted this book to study or to present to my university class. I didn't actually have to say that – as long as I was pretending it to myself, I could walk up to her desk and ask for the book.

"I'm looking for a book by Loren Cameron," I announced, my head up, my eyes focused, daring her to find me repulsive. "It's called *Body Alchemy*."

She was white haired and hunched in her paisley-patterned dress, and I was embarrassed that I was subjecting her to this. But she didn't know yet. She punched at the computer keys.

"Oh, here it is," she said brightly. "Let's see. It's down in the photographer section – first floor. Just tell them you want ..." She put a finger to the screen and read aloud as it moved along the words. "Tell them you want *Body Alchemy: Transsexu –*" She stopped reading for a moment, then fluttered her hand in the air. "Oh, just tell them it's a softcover."

I was done telling anyone anything. I found the book myself and stood in line for several fretful minutes, afraid again that sirens would go off and lights would flash when I got up to the checkout. "Oh, a transgender person," the clerk would say, flashing the book around for everyone to see. "Come over here a minute, Martha. Here's a transgender person." But he didn't, and I slipped through a side door to the safety of the street.

Outside, I settled on a bench and pulled the book out, trying to hold it so that all the passersby, who surely had a personal interest in what I was reading, couldn't see it. Loren Cameron's photographs were all of men who had transitioned from female to male, and it included his own self-portraits.

The "Before and After" pictures featured good-looking,

sturdy women who had become good-looking, sturdy men. They were confident women in those photographs – they were sure then of who they were and what they wanted and what they would become. They were so unlike me. How many of them had reeked of sweat after going in just to buy a book? How many of them had circled a building in panic before going in for a meeting?

Almost all of them, but I didn't know that then. I only knew that what I saw was something completely foreign to me, something that simply didn't exist in the mainstream, heterosexual, two-gendered world that I had lived in thus far. But it did exist – *they* existed, in some parallel universe that I would eventually enter and that would come to seem more normal to me than the one I left.

And even further down the road, I would realize that trans people did not exist in a parallel universe after all, but in the same universe as everyone else, with different and more broadly defined dimensions.

This is a universe where genders can blur or stand out in stark contrast and either is okay. It's a world of liberation, both for trans and non-trans people, because there are no gender expectations. Whoever you are and whatever you do can be male, female, or simply human. You finally have a chance to breathe.

This isn't some exclusive world. Anyone can get there, trans or not. All it takes is eliminating some outmoded ideas about gender. All it takes is crossing that invisible safety barrier at the edge of the street and realizing that sirens won't go off, news reporters won't descend, and the world will look pretty much the same way that it did before, with one exception – now you're free.

My Father's Purse

THE FIRST AND only time I saw my father carrying a purse, I was still in shaky recovery from that stage of life where your parents can embarrass you just by retrieving the morning paper. In high school, I always prayed that none of my friends was driving by at 6 a.m. on Sunday morning when my father stepped outside in his plaid shorts, black over-the-calf socks, and sandals to bring in the Sunday *Times*.

But my father was fifty at the time of the purse incident, and I was twenty-one. I thought that I had outgrown my adolescent shame about the fact that my parents existed at all – until I saw my father toting that tote.

It was a campus weekend, like many others, filled with planned activities that let me believe that I was heading into adulthood while forgetting that my parents were footing the bill. And this one featured a particularly sophisticated event – a jazz concert in the park that promised to draw hordes of hip students who, like me, had stretched the umbilical cord to the snapping point, and who occasionally liked to let it snap back, but not in front of anyone else.

My parents had come to visit me that weekend, and their visits were not always a bad thing. They usually brought care packages filled with chocolate chip cookies and little gifts, they took me out to eat, and handed me money when they left. They were pleasant enough to be around, and I rarely had to exert myself in their presence. We got along – almost, but not quite yet, on the level of adult equals.

This time, however, there was a problem – the concert. The mere mention of jazz would transport my parents back in time, morphing them into non-parents, real people who had lives that were completely independent of any parenting roles they had later signed on for. They would be at the park, and there wasn't much I could do to stop them.

Getting money and cookies was fine, as was sitting in a darkened restaurant, allowing them to listen to the unending struggles and unbearable traumas that made up university life. But the jazz concert was real life, in the light of day, with friends and strangers and the musty odor of marijuana mingling with the scent of secret spices from open tubs of Kentucky Fried Chicken.

It was men dressed in dashikis who had never been to Africa and women in peasant dresses who had never been peasants. It was half-empty wine jugs passed from person to person and a "share the land" philosophy that gave everyone a chance to rebel against society while still fitting in with everyone else – unless their parents were there.

They had no intention of sitting with me. They came to hear jazz, and at that point, they were probably just as eager to separate themselves from me as I was to declare my independence from them. But no matter how far away from me they sat, no matter how many people were huddled in bunches between their blanket and mine, I knew they were there. And I knew that, at any moment, there was the chance that they would do something in front of my friends and the whole campus to completely humiliate me.

But even my worst-case scenario – that they would get up and dance – was nothing compared to the reality that confronted me when I looked up and saw my father walking across the grass and heading straight toward my friends and me.

He was clutching a brown leather purse in his fingertips, his hands dangling, limp wristed, in front of him, and he appeared utterly unconcerned about the connotations of this act or about the fact that his handbag didn't match his shoes and belt. At that moment, I would have traded that purse in for the plaid shorts and black socks without a whimper. Everyone there understood the concept of father-as-nerd. But very few – including me – understood the concept of father-as-mother.

Gender roles had always been pretty well defined in our household. My father worked in an office, my mother stayed home and raised children. He cut the grass, she cleaned the house. He drove the car, she rode shotgun, with the kids in the back like a '60s public service commercial for seat belts. He paid the bills – with money from his *wallet*. My mother and I carried the purses, with the money in them that my father earned "at the office."

This was the way the world worked – at least my world, and I was only vaguely aware at the time that there might be others. But even if there were, it made sense that they would adhere to something so basic as the unwavering Western gender system. Men were men. Women were women. And everyone knew which one wore the pants in the family – and which one accessorized.

It was true that, occasionally, my father played fast and loose with the culture's expectations, but it seemed to me to be a private matter, not open for societal inspection. He was the only man I knew who owned a candy thermometer – or at least who would admit to it. He was the only man I knew who liked to spend his Saturdays baking bread and doughnuts. He went with my mother to PTA meetings and school open houses, he helped organize little-girl birthday parties and even stuck around for them, and he loved planning holiday surprises. Women things.

He fretted about the problems of his friends, who always seemed comfortable confiding in him, and he took turns with my mother getting up in the middle of the night when I was sick. Caretaking. Female things.

Thus far, he had managed to temper most of his feminine qualities by partaking in such masculine activities as opening the hood of the car and looking inside, tugging at various wires and unscrewing caps. If he got a little grease on his sweatshirt, so much the better – it disguised the white patches of flour from a morning in the kitchen and reintroduced the masculine aura that had been lost inside so many measuring cups.

He did watch football, he occasionally went fishing, and he was in the Navy at one point in his life, but so were the Village People – or at least they sang about it like they knew what they were talking about. And now, he had apparently taken to carrying a purse.

This purse was not even the style of the season. Anyone in the know was carrying a Kenya bag, although no one I knew had ever been to Kenya. A Kenya bag was a huge sack of a bag made of intricately woven threads of various colors and designs. It was a handy depository for all things feminine, and of course, only a woman would carry one. A purse as a prop was in the female domain. It symbolized womanhood in a way that few things – besides breasts – ever could. It was a primary delineator of the genders, and my father was making a mockery of everything that it stood for – and humiliating me in the process.

As I watched him winding through the crowd with his pocketbook, the separation of gender roles and what constituted "normal" male and female behavior was very clear in my mind. My stomach tightened, my breath quickened, and I felt angry and ashamed.

As he got closer, I turned away, but it was too late. He could always recognize me in a crowd. Another few seconds and he was there, for all the world to see, looming over my friends and me with his trendy little handbag. I had to look. And when I did, I saw that there was something hidden behind the handbag – a book, a gift that he had brought for a friend of mine, just because he knew my friend would like it.

The purse was my mother's, and he had grabbed it so he could hide the book as he approached. It hadn't occurred to him that even in the simple act of carrying that purse, he was traversing a well-established gender boundary – or he just didn't care.

My friend was delighted with the book. She didn't care how it got there. But I did. This special gift, one man's thoughtfulness, was overshadowed by the only thing that I could see – my father weaving his way back across the park with a purse in his hand.

Twenty-three years later, I was standing in the lobby of a Unitarian church, watching wedding guests file out and waiting for the happy couple. Nothing seemed unusual – not the fact that the bride, who was resplendent in a flowing princess gown with a plunging neckline that highlighted her small, round breasts, was assigned male at birth. Not the fact that the other bride, who was assigned female at birth and remained so, was dressed in a medieval man's outfit reminiscent of Robin Hood. Not the fact that the majority of women in attendance, in their high heels, hose, and festive finery, all had original birth certificates that identified them as baby boys. Not the fact that the majority of men in attendance were there with their dates, who were also men.

Nothing seemed unusual – until my friend asked me to hold her purse.

"Just for a minute," she said. "I'm going to get some food. Men hold women's purses. That's what they do. You're going to have to have to learn that now."

But it was too much – even just for a minute. She came back to find her purse stashed behind a chair. I am not my father.

One of the first things that I did when I decided I was going to transition – even before I cut my hair and gave up makeup – was ditch my purse. My new wallet rode conveniently in my back pocket. Just slipping that wallet into and out of my pocket seemed utterly masculine and became a frequent, almost obsessive, activity for a while. That wallet defined my manhood for me. At the time, it was one of the few things that did. I am not my father.

My father is dead. He died four years after he smuggled my friend's gift across the park behind that purse. I don't think the two were related, although I realize now how many deaths in this world might be the result of just such a thing – a "man" carrying a purse, a person adopting the visible accessories of a gender that doesn't match what the world sees and what the world expects from that person.

Somehow, my father got away with it – probably because he didn't rely on outer trappings, or other people, to tell him who he was. But I hadn't learned that lesson yet, and he wasn't there to teach me. I was still struggling to define myself by what I saw and by what I knew the world to be.

I didn't know how to tie a tie. I didn't know how to change a flat tire, and I could barely open a car hood and tug at wires and unscrew caps. Men things. I started out trying to do those things on my own. I bought books so I could learn how to dress like a man, and I carefully followed the diagrams that demonstrated tie tying. I fumbled, I cursed, and I choked. I watched other men, and I learned to stand with my legs apart, to shove my hands in my pockets, to take on a façade of masculinity, because there was no one there to show me how it worked from the inside out. I swaggered and I swore and I struggled for a role model. And then I realized that I had one.

The ties went into the back of the closet and I came out of it – out of the binary gender system and into the transgender world, where none of the rules had to apply. When some of your best friends are women who can write their name in the snow or men who can recount their labor pains, the thought of a man carrying a purse eventually doesn't even make a blip on your weirdness radar screen.

Watching men with full beards strap down their breasts and balding women stuff their bras becomes commonplace. I no longer see the Adam's apples, the snakelike veins, the muscular shoulders, or the five o'clock shadows on some of the women I know – those things simply aren't there, or if they are, they seem natural. I don't notice the rounded hips, the short stature, the small hands and feet, or the baby-smooth faces on some of the men I know – it's just one more way for a man to look. When gender boundaries start to blur, there are no men things anymore, and no women things. There are only human things.

It isn't something that happens overnight. I took a long journey to get to that place, and it can't be imposed on someone at will. But I like to think that trans people will be the catalysts for a cultural shift that will result in everyone's liberation. And I like to think that maybe my father was just ahead of his time – one of the earliest specimens of a liberated man.

I still haven't tried the doughnut recipe my father left me as his legacy. Since I never learned to cook, I'd probably screw it up and be less of a man because of it. Or less of a woman.

Or something. I don't know anymore and it doesn't make any difference. If my father were still alive, I could ask him how to make the doughnuts, and then I could ask him how to be a son, because I never quite got there either. He wouldn't recognize me now, across a crowded park, but I'd know that purse anywhere.

And this time, I'd stand up and wave, call him over and ask him to sit down. We could talk about man things or woman things or people things, and we'd probably both have plenty to add to the conversation.

And before he got up and walked away, carrying that little purse out in front of him with both his hands, I'd say, "Hey, Dad. That long strap hanging down? It goes on your shoulder." And then he'd probably thank me, hitch it up, and walk away across the park, happily swinging his shoulder bag and looking very much like the man – the person – that he was, and that I can only aspire to be.

Constipation

IT'S 8 P.M. on a Friday, and I'm sitting in a strange emergency medical clinic in a strange suburb waiting to see a strange doctor for a condition that's embarrassing just to write on the intake form, let alone formally announce – even to a medical professional. The scientific term for my ailment is, I believe, constipation, but that simple word fails to even touch upon the excruciating fullness that begins at my diaphragm, seems to end about an inch below my butt cheeks, and has refused to budge. I'm plugged up, backed up, in pain that runs from moderate to severe depending on my body position, and maybe facing overnight extinction without some serious intervention.

Which is why I'm sitting in this waiting room examining the tiny square pattern in the linoleum floor and pretending to read a magazine article about Britney Spears and her marriage or her baby or her secret love or something that she did that has no bearing on real life as anyone knows it. I occasionally glance sideways at the man a few seats down with an ankle the size of a child's bowling ball, or the woman next to him with a possible broken arm who possibly doesn't have insurance and who will probably not get seen because of it. I'm lucky, I guess. I have insurance. I will get seen. And I can walk without dragging my ankle behind me as if I were a prisoner on a chain gang. But even so, I wish my malady were something that could be treated while my clothes were still on.

I have already completed the first hurdle of the evening,

which involved casually writing "Constipation – bad" on the intake form and returning it to the young receptionist, trying to act as though my ankle were sprained or my arm were broken or I had some other normal complaint that wouldn't involve a bare rear end and potential smelliness. It was hard to make eye contact with her when I handed back the clipboard, so I chose instead to struggle with the pen on its little chain, trying to get it hooked correctly into place, as if this were a major patient responsibility that had to be completed before I could be seen. Then I strolled back to my seat and tried to become engrossed in Britney's life.

I finally look up long enough to see the two male doctors on duty scuttle around behind the counter, then disappear into rooms and behind curtains with other patients, and I try to get a sense of whether or not they will flip a coin over the plugged-up guy or if one owes the other a gambling debt and will finally be able to pay it off just by agreeing to treat me. No matter how it goes, somebody's going to lose. I hope it's not me.

I had tried to avoid this inevitability. I have my own doctor who I see for regular medical care, who is already "broken in" and knows what she's going to find – or not find – underneath the men's clothing, and I had decided earlier in the week that if things got too bad, I could eventually go to my general practitioner. But I was going to try my own remedies first. So all week, I had gulped down gummy fiber drinks, popped cheap laxative pills, and then, in a last ditch effort to avoid the crisis that was looming, I stopped at the grocery store after work and bought an enema.

Just buying the enema was torture in itself, and I had to scramble to find some other things that I needed as well. That way, I could shove the enema into the bottom of my shopping cart and cover it with boxes of cereal that I probably wouldn't eat, magazines that I probably wouldn't read, and a big bag of puffy marshmallows that would stay in my cupboard until they got hard and I threw them away.

But the real torture came after I got home, and it wasn't just in realizing how much money I wasted to cover up one little item. The box instructed me to get into the bathtub on my knees, a feat that is almost impossible to accomplish once you've hit fifty and your knees become a useless body part. And after I managed to get into this poor excuse for a fetal position, I was then supposed to reach around behind myself and insert said enema into a place that I not only couldn't reach, but that I prefer not to acknowledge at all. After pulling a shoulder muscle and twisting my wrist, I finally managed to find the entry point I was looking for, but all my efforts seemed to be in vain – the entry point was blocked.

Nothing was going to happen. My attempts at home remedies had accomplished nothing other than to create a Friday-night emergency, forcing me to leave the comfort of the city limits, where "gender variance" is legally protected from discrimination, and drive to an after-hours clinic in the suburbs, where, for all I knew, it could be opening day of "gender variance" hunting season.

I continue to take surreptitious glances behind the counter at the two doctors, trying to figure out from the way they move or style their hair which one might be wearing the cross of the Evangelical Church of Physical Conformity under his scrubs. Some of the outlying areas of Colorado tend toward the dangerous side. There are people in this state who would pay a steep admission fee and spring for a box of overpriced popcorn just to watch a transsexual person slowly succumb to the poison of his own undigested frozen dinners, and then shake their head, cluck their tongue, and say, "That's what happens when you go against God's plan." As if discrimination leading to death were part of God's plan – let alone frozen dinners.

But it doesn't matter. I don't have a choice. And regardless of the prevailing notions outside the liberal enclave in which I live, I'm just as human as the guy with the severely deformed ankle, and I have just as much right to treatment as the woman with the possibly broken arm – more right, as it turns out, because she is sent away for having no insurance. I wonder if the current crop of conservatives in my state and in this country finds a transsexual person with an insurance card in his pocket more deserving of medical care than a non-trans person without one. I decide the answer is obvious as I watch her struggle out the door, cradling the errant arm.

But I'm distracting myself. My continued call for universal health insurance will have to recommence after I see whether or not one person – me – can regain his health tonight, and whether or not a transsexual person will be worthy of a cure.

The one thing I notice about this bustling group of medical professionals is that everyone seems to be alarmingly cheerful. It's a Friday night, their friends and family are all comfortably at home or out having a fun-filled time without them, they still have to treat an ankle and an intestine that are both increasing exponentially in size, and they seem to be enjoying every minute of it. Even the man with the swollen ankle, now limping like Jack Nicholson in *The Shining* as he's led into the examination area, has perked up and is happily recounting the details of his injury.

Watching the general merriment, I start to feel an increasing anxiety. I worry that I'm going to be the spoiler. They already know that someone is going to be sacrificed in the excavation of my netherparts – that has so far not dampened their spirits. What they don't know is that there is a transsexual person in their waiting room. This could change the entire dynamic. I simply don't know yet, and that's one of the problems that seems to be inherent in transsexuality – you never really know.

You never really know what word, what action, what revelation might alter the entire situation that you're in at any given moment and what the consequences might be. You are simply left to wonder, to shift and worry in your chair, to expect the worst and hope for the best.

A young, blonde, and chipper nurse finally leads my aching, bloated body through the door, past the doctors, and into an examination room. Some people just get a table with a curtain pulled around it, right out in the center of the treatment area, but apparently my particular ailment deserves the privacy of a full-fledged room with a closing door. And they don't even know the half of it yet.

Her nametag says "Tiffany," and it's a perfect young name, signaling a new and improved generation of nurses, which is probably why she's plucky and perky and eager to take my temperature and blood pressure. I hope that she doesn't have to stay in the room for the examination – not so much because of my strikingly unexpected genitalia, which she sees in similar form on herself every day of her life, but because I really don't want anyone named Tiffany examining my rear or anything else related to my current situation.

"Well, Mr. Kailey," she says as she picks up her clipboard and starts for the door. "Everything's fine so far. The doctor will be in shortly."

And that's when I stop her. I've already rehearsed my speech in my head, but I don't know what it will sound like when it comes out. I don't know if she will "get" it. But there are times when I feel as if preparation is essential – as if surprises just aren't going to be fun for anyone involved – and so I need to lay the groundwork. I don't know if I'm protecting the ill-fated doctor or myself, but I suspect it's me, and I know I'll be even more vulnerable when I'm lying on my side in a fetal position with the doctor's face inches away from my impacted butt and my inconsistent body parts.

"I need to see the more open-minded of the two doctors," I say to Tiffany, "because he won't see what he expects to see when he examines me. What I mean is, I don't have the parts he'll be expecting."

I shrug and try to be casual. I try to impart to Tiffany that this is no big deal, that I'm only telling her because everyone has some disclaimer and this is mine and somebody should know. And I wait for the deer-in-headlights stare or the embarrassed shifting or the quickly lowered eyes. But what I expect to happen does not. Tiffany's facial expression does not change. Her smile does not become strained. No tiny furrow develops on her brow. She simply smiles and says, "Well, either one, I think, will be fine, but I'll tell them."

Who trains these people? I picture a stout, middle-aged professor of nursing telling her young charges, "Now remember, not everyone has genitalia that matches the rest of them. Don't act surprised. When confronted with this situation, use your 'I secretly know you're dying, but I'm going to act like everything's fine' face." Tiffany would be at the top of her game in an intensive care unit someplace – or playing poker in Vegas.

After she leaves, I am alone – for quite some time. I don't know what she's told the doctors, and there's a possibility that they're now arm wrestling to see who has to treat me. I finally decide that they've simply all gone home to their spouses and partners who *do* have the genitalia that they expect to see, and left me safely locked in for the night so I can't infiltrate their schools, their churches, or their neighborhoods with my transsexual agenda. But no. Finally Dr. Michaels enters – mid-forties, black glasses, boisterously cheerful, as if examining rear ends and dealing with unusual genitalia are the things that make his job come alive for him.

And it is odd to be facing him. The feeling is not exactly discomfort, but something akin to dysphoria or disengagement – the feeling that I get when I am talking to an adult man, someone with whom I'm supposed to have things in common. There is a sense that we are not meeting on equal footing, as two guys born and raised in the halls of the men's club, but that we are talking across some kind of a chasm that can't be bridged.

I have yet to see myself as one of them – these men who move through the world as if they belong to it, and it to them, so easy in their dealings with life and with each other. And it is usually made more complicated by the fact that they look at me and don't see the chasm. They think they are talking to one of their own. They expect certain responses, certain movements, certain nods, expressions, and gestures – *and I don't know what they are.*

I'm not one of you, I think, but Dr. Michaels must know that, if Tiffany talked to him. But then I realize that I was cryptic with Tiffany. I didn't say "I'm transsexual" to her, and I don't say it now. In that room with glaring florescent lights, clean and sterile and devoid of the soft, rounded edges that can sometimes absorb a word like this, it seems to me that "transsexual," said out loud, would hang there between us in the brightly lit room, as impersonal and clinical as the blood pressure machine dangling at the head of the examination table or the glass canister of cotton swabs on the counter.

"Did the nurse tell you about me?" I ask. "Because I'm not going to have the parts that you would expect to see when you get down there."

"Down there" are the words of a child, and I begin to understand that the chasm that I sometimes feel in the company of grown men is the gap between childhood and adulthood, the large, empty space that is filled, for them, with the experience of living an entire life as a man, and that, for me, is left gaping and void. My guess is that I'm older than Dr. Michaels, but at this moment, that fact seems to account for nothing at all – at least not to me. Dr. Michaels, however, seems unconcerned – about my age, my gender, or what he might find when he finally gets "down there."

He grins and peers at me through his glasses. "I've been in this business for fifteen years," he says proudly. "There's *nothing* I haven't seen."

I doubt that. But I feel an instant sense of relief. There are times when I'm prepared to be defiant about my transsexuality, to battle it out with whoever objects and demand the treatment that I deserve just by virtue of my status as a human being – but now, when I'm tired and plugged up and even a tiny bit scared, is not one of those times. Tonight I am made vulnerable by illness and by difference. Tonight I want unconditional acceptance without having to ask for it and certainly without having to demand it. And I feel lucky that I'm conscious and lucid and can make my own decisions, and that I can at least give Dr. Michaels a heads up about what he's going to find, even if I haven't made myself completely clear.

But he's game for the challenge. He assures me that he's unplugged hundreds of butts, which makes me believe that there's *almost* nothing he hasn't seen, and I try hard not to conjure up the pictures of everything he *has* seen.

I lie on my side with my legs pulled up and a cloth drape covering everything but the problem area, which is the one place that I really wish were covered. He pokes around for a minute as I brace myself for some jaw-clenching discomfort, but he can't find anything. There's nothing blocking the exit.

"There's nothing much here," he says to my rear, and I think about how true that statement is on so many levels. "Well, we'll have to get an x-ray so we can see what's going on."

So now I must get dressed for x-rays, and even though it's after 9 p.m. and time for everyone to go home, they are all more than happy to stay and take on the challenge of clearing my plumbing. The x-ray technician is joyful, and even Tiffany is still smiling. Maybe they're all waiting to see if my insides are as convoluted as my outsides.

And they are, in a way. What I lack on the outside is more than made up for by the extra junk inside. My intestine is full, and as we examine the x-ray together, Dr. Michaels shows me where my last fifteen meals have taken permanent refuge. But although my full intestines are slightly interesting, what really fascinates me is the x-ray itself – my body, up there on a lighted screen, the spinal cord running almost vertically up the photograph, my intestines, full or not, curving across the picture like a giant boa constrictor underneath my stomach and my heart. It's no different from any other body.

I've seen my own x-rays before, but this one strikes me in a particularly unusual way – both humbling and gratifying. The humbling part is that I'm really not exceptional – this is just a body that will deteriorate and die, like any other. It's not stronger, it's not of greater value – it's interchangeable. It could be anyone.

And that is also the gratifying part. As Dr. Michaels examines the x-ray with me, pointing out the shading and patchy areas that signify my major problem, I realize that he's looked at hundreds, maybe thousands, of these pictures, and with only minor variations that indicate some personal pathology, they are all the same. The x-ray of my body is probably very similar to his own. And although it may be true that there's nothing he hasn't seen – and after tonight, I'm sure of that – what he really sees is what's on the picture in front of him.

He sees a mortal, fallible, everyday, average human being. You can't get much more banal than that. All that worry. All that fear. And all that happens is that I am eventually sent away, into the darkness of the night and my own self-imposed paranoia, with a prescription for a special liquid to drink that will clean me out and a hearty "Good night" from the doctor and the staff.

The stars are visible in this suburb. They aren't muted or blocked from view by the closer and competing lights of the city. There are thousands of them, glittering across the sky, and I know they all have names, but I don't know which is which. How could I tell them apart? They all seem exactly the same.

When I saw *The Exorcist* for the first time, in college, I couldn't sleep for days, so certain was I that I would be Satan's next victim. When I told my father how scared I was that I was next up on the Devil's list for possession, he just looked at me, raised his eyebrows, and said, "Do you really think you're that special?"

Indeed.

Putting the Men in Menopause

SHORTLY AFTER I turned fifty, I started to perspire. It wasn't the glowy dew that I had produced as a female and it wasn't the labor-intensive, manly sweat that I like to think comes naturally to a hard-working, macho man who sits behind a desk and types for a living. It started at the top of my head and crept its way down, as if I had slowly stepped into a sauna, head first and then body part by body part, activating sweat glands that I didn't even know I possessed, until I was left soggy and soaking, my clothes tattooed to my sticky, wet body. It was nature turning a hose on me as if I were some hormone-crazed dog.

This happened whether I was sitting on a blanket in the sun or directly in front of an air-conditioner turned on at full blast. It happened in bed and it happened on the street. It took me a while to realize that not every place I went was mysteriously undergoing random temperature fluctuations. This was internal – my own personal global warming.

The worst thing about these episodes was that they had a scary emotional component that often went with them. This part happened primarily at night, when things are scarier anyway, when I already found myself lying awake for hours wondering what hideous rare disease I was going to die from, how I was going to pay my bills until that time, and what exactly was going to happen to me when the universe stopped expanding and started to fold back in on itself.

As I pondered these things, a new and unfamiliar feeling

crept over me – one of imminent dread and doom, as if some-thing were horribly wrong *right at that moment* and I just didn't know about it yet. Maybe the universe was folding in on itself already, and it would all get back to where I was before the flesh-eating-mad-cow-avian-flu caught up to me.

Then, within a minute or five, the wave of heat began moving down my body, inch by inch, or sometimes millime-ter by millimeter. I could feel it beginning at the roots of my hair, creeping down my face and neck, across my chest, down my stomach and legs, and out the bottoms of my feet. Then it was all over, leaving a trail of sweat, and a resulting chill, in its wake. It was so powerful an experience that, even when I had managed to fall asleep in spite of all the worldly threats out there, it woke me up to lie shivering in my own perspiration.

It took about a week for me to realize what was happen-ing. At work, I complained when the air-conditioning vent in my office was open. I complained when it was closed. It was too hot, it was too cold, it was just right, and none of it was right. How could everyone else be comfortable when my skin was literally drowning, my heart was racing, and I was trapped in this rapid climate change that I couldn't control or understand?

If my coworkers couldn't experience what I was going through, at least they could suffer vicariously by listening to me whine. And once I finally realized what it was all about, I felt utterly justified in my complaint. After all, how many men reach across their desk for a stack of papers to use as a fan, come to a sudden "aha" moment, stand up, and announce to their colleagues, "That's what it is – I'm going through menopause."

The words came tumbling out of my mouth with a mixture of awe and pride, as if I'd just received notification that I'd won an award – not some Publisher's Clearinghouse Sweepstakes, but an award that I had actually done something to deserve. It was as if this unexpected physiological phenomenon were a goal that I had personally worked for and finally achieved – a biological personal best.

Perhaps it was the memory of my mother's pride when I got my first period that made me unashamed to announce to everyone that what had started so many years ago in that bathroom had finally come full circle. Despite all the changes that my body had undergone during transition, it was somehow still in possession of its original operating instructions. I had done it – I had finally ended what I started back in sixth grade. I had finished the world's longest marathon – the 50k Fertility Fun Run.

At the time, I worked with a bunch of gay guys who had turned self-absorbed whining into an art form, along with some hip young lesbians who would eventually go through womynopause, so they at least took the whole thing in stride. Working side by side with a transsexual person can be a bit of a novelty, so the price they paid for putting up with the odd developments in my life was worth having a good story to tell at home. And the price I paid for working with a bunch of gay guys and young lesbians is that my menopausal symptoms got no sympathy.

In fact, nobody there even knew what I was talking about. My twenty-something officemate eventually procured a fan to put by my desk, but I'm not sure whether she did it to be kind, to make me stop sighing heavily, or to blow the unpleasant stench of my sweating body in another direction.

The irony of the whole thing was that menopause couldn't have been a better word for my situation. Whatever manhood I actually possessed had been put on hold, as if a giant pause button had been pushed on my life. Some people say that we are humans having a spiritual experience, and others say that we are spirits having a human experience, both of which are very high-minded and ethereal – but they are nothing compared to a man having a female experience.

It's not that this had never happened to me before – I had female experiences for the first forty-two years of my life. It's just that I had breasts then, and no facial hair. I wore high-heels, beaded earrings, and lipstick, and female experiences were expected of me. Women actually commiserated with me, and I with them, over makeup disasters and menstrual cramps and missed periods – all of which could be equally catastrophic, depending on the circumstances.

Now I had no one to share my misery. The gay guys looked at me blankly, blinked once or twice, and turned back to their computers to look at their pornographic screensavers. The young lesbians, possibly seeing me as some sort of harbinger of their distant and scary future, all decided to go en masse to the gym. Even my trans men friends outside of work didn't want to hear about it – it was too much a reminder of their own histories, too much of a "there but for the grace of God go I" kind of thing.

And I could hardly lean over the counter at the drug store, start fanning myself, and say to the middle-aged salesclerk, "Oh, these hot flashes are killing me." Where once she might have clucked her tongue and given me some sisterly advice, now she would back up slowly and reach for the alarm button. I was in it alone, going through something that men don't go through and that I somehow had to come to terms with. My body was doing what it pleased, what it was programmed to do, and I had to step aside and allow nature to take its course.

I eventually figured out why it was happening – I had let my testosterone levels get too low. I don't have an internal factory creating the stuff, and my own internal factory, without a regularly administered dose of the hormone, had turned into a sweatshop.

But in many ways, I didn't mind. I didn't like the hot flashes and I didn't like the sensation of impending doom, the waves of nausea, or the general feeling of crappiness that sometimes accompanied all of it, but I had a remedy that most menopausal people don't have – I could increase my testosterone dose until some semblance of manliness kicked back in.

And I didn't mind because it was all part of being transsexual. It was just one more damned interesting aspect of a life that's been shaped by the oddities and the unpredictability of nature. It was just one more way to understand the world, looking out from a body that's straddling the fence, and to see how wild and wonderful this thing called life really is. The pride and awe that I felt came from possessing a body that wasn't totally my possession, that was part of the universal flow of things, and that sometimes had its own agenda, and the most that I could do was stand back and watch and shake my head in wonderment.

And I didn't mind because it was humbling, in a way that let me know where I stand with nature and with the universe, that let me know that there are some things more powerful than I am, some things that I simply can't control.

I have a transsexual body, and the things that I now deal with in my everyday life are the result of the choices that I have made coupled with powers beyond my reach. Nature is strong, and no matter how much testosterone I take and how many biceps curls I manage, I will never be stronger. Although I know a lot of trans men who would be appalled at going through menopause, and even more appalled at actually talking about it, for me, the acceptance of what nature is going to do, whether I like it or not, and the ability to talk about it have been saviors of my sanity. So I'll keep talking.

Is it hot in here, or is it just me?

Just Your Average Fetish Call

THE LITTLE RED message light on my work phone is on, and since that rarely happens, it can mean only one thing – that I have an annoying or bizarre message that no one else in the office knows how to handle. I'm reluctant to check it out, but my employer pays me in the hope that I'll carry out my job responsibilities, so I pick up the phone and push the five to seven secret codes that allow me access to a message that proves to be both annoying *and* bizarre.

"They transferred me to you because they thought you could help me," says a soft and nasally male voice. "I'm looking for a transsexual to date and possibly marry."

Of course. These are always the calls that get transferred to me.

But today is not the day for this particular message. Today is one of my "I hate being transsexual" days, which are rare, but always emotionally complicated by the fact that I hate having "I hate being transsexual" days. They make me feel guilty, because on these certain days, my hatred at being transsexual stems not from job or housing discrimination, being harassed or assaulted on the street, having my family and friends desert me, or being arrested for no reason and charged with impersonating a human being. My hatred stems from the most superficial of traumas.

First of all, I'm going bald. Okay, not in a major way, like my friends who are perfecting the art of the comb-over or who have given up entirely and just shaved their head, but every morning there are more and more hairs in the sink and fewer and fewer hairs on the back of my head. Today is one of the few days that I decided to pay attention to this fact, and I spent an extra ten minutes examining my scalp with the Mary Kay compact mirror that's a holdover from my girl days. When my friends come over, I try to remember to hide it in the back of the medicine cabinet, but it's very handy to see places that you normally can't see, and I don't carry it with me. That's one concession to masculinity I've made.

So I'm going bald and this wasn't supposed to happen to me, but since it's happening *behind* me, I can put down my Mary Kay mirror and ignore it for a little while. Unfortunately, I can't ignore my hips, because they're happening on every side of me. I usually just pull on a pair of pants and forget about it, but today I was already obsessed with finding fault, so every pair of pants that I put on seemed to scream, "Get me off these female hips. Go have a baby, honey, and quit trying to fool everybody by shopping in the men's department."

I was a balding guy with wide hips, shoving on a pair of shoes from the boy's department at Payless and schlepping out the door, feeling like I had a sign on my back that said, "Kick me. I'm transsexual." I wanted to start over, in some other body, in some other life, but instead I had to go to work, where I have now been given the major responsibility of handling this urgent message.

I'm used to handling weird phone calls. At the LGBT newspaper where I work, everyone is responsible for answering the phone when it rings, and at least half of the calls have nothing to do with the actual business of newspapering. We're the clearinghouse, the information center, and the lifeline for anyone in the community who needs a phone number, a fantasy, a date – or, apparently, a wife.

I've talked to people who want to know "where the black guys hang out," as if there's a secret club. I've read sensual massage ads out loud in a businesslike manner while trying desperately to block out the picture of what was happening on the other end of the line. It's not easy to say "Studly, well-hung master will satisfy your every fantasy with a steamy full-body rubdown" in the same voice that I use to tell someone where to send a press release. I've hunted down phone numbers to other gay establishments, recited the merits of various bars, described escort photos to blind men ("Well, yeah, he's good looking, but it depends on what you like. He does have nice abs."), and commiserated with those who felt discriminated against for getting a parking ticket – "Yes, it could have been the rainbow flag on the car, but the fact that you were blocking the driveway of a fire station might have figured into it." And then there are the ones who are "looking for a transsexual."

My coworkers believe that I'm the expert in this area. The fact that I haven't had a date of my own since the turn of the century (the twenty-first, not the twentieth) doesn't seem to negate their belief that I know the perfect "trolling for trans" spots in town and that I'm happy to act as a matchmaker for anyone who calls in with this particular desire. It's as if all the transsexual people in Denver congregate at one particular end of one particular bar on Wednesday nights at 7:21 p.m., and if you're looking for one, well, I recommend that you get there early to nab your place in line. Bring a snack.

My first reaction to this message is to slam down the phone and loudly announce, "We're a newspaper, not a dating service." Getting no response from anyone within earshot, I gripe, "Why do I always get these calls?" No response. Before I have a chance to think of another retort, the phone rings, someone answers, and it's for me. I know it's him. He couldn't even wait for me to call him back. Hey, when you want a transsexual, you want a transsexual, I guess. So now I have to handle this call.

The poor guy doesn't know that I'm having an "I hate being transsexual" day. He doesn't even know that I *am* transsexual, and he may not know that female-to-male transsexuals exist. All the "trolling for trans" callers that I've ever dealt with are men looking for trans women, and they assume that, just by saying the word "transsexual," everyone will know this. So now I am not only big-hipped and bald with little-boy feet, but I am invisible as well.

I try to withhold judgment and keep the anger out of my voice, but it is impossible. After I give him the names of a couple of bars, which it turns out he has already tried, and suggest some online dating services, which he has already pursued, I finally lose it – but only slightly. I am, after all, representing not myself, but my newspaper – and, apparently, transsexual people everywhere, as well.

"I wouldn't bring up the marriage thing right away if I were you," I say, and I feel the blood rising to my face, and with it, a surge of anger that I try to force down. "It's just that when you say, 'I'm looking for a transsexual to date and marry,' it really sounds like you don't care much about the person, that you're only interested in a body – any body, as long as it's a transsexual body. That really isn't very attractive to most people."

He's mortified, and he apologizes over and over again. It's just that transsexuals are so nice, he says. They're so friendly and so much fun. They're so kind and gentle and caring. *Not all of them, buddy.* Maybe it's the estrogen that makes the objects of his desire as cute and cuddly as a newborn lamb, and maybe it's the testosterone that makes me want to reach through the phone and pocket his balls for objectifying the females of my species, but in spite of my irritation, I feel a little sorry for the guy.

There are so many times when I've gone back and forth myself on this very issue, and more than once, I have argued for exactly his position – not that transsexual people are so nice and fun and all (I know more than a few who wouldn't hold up under close scrutiny), but that it's okay to have a preference, that it's okay to like a certain "type" over some other "type," and that "trans-chasers" are only expressing a personal preference for a particular body type or history or physical appearance.

The people with whom I have argued this point insist that those who are interested in transsexual people on the sheer basis of their transsexuality are fetishists. They might be sick, they might be perverted, and they are, at the very least, weird. "I don't want some guy going out with me because he thinks it's cool to date a man without a penis," said one reluctant trans guy during a discussion. And I understand his position – on the one hand.

On the other hand, what's the difference between someone being attracted to me because of my current body composition and someone who was attracted to me in my previous incarnation as a female because I had boobs and a vagina and long hair? Isn't that what attraction is all about – a particular look, a particular body, a particular set of sexual organs, a particular way of living and moving through the world?

There seems to be a fine line between attraction and fetish, and a lurking, though unacknowledged, possibility that the two could be synonyms. Regardless, we are not always responsible for what turns us on and who we fall for. This is why sexual orientation is not a choice, why people go to certain places and not others to meet potential partners, and why people put physical characteristics – both their own and those that they are looking for – in personal ads. Maybe it's okay to be what we are and accept the admiration that we get for it. Or maybe I should remain offended. I'm simply not sure anymore.

But none of this is helping the poor guy on the other end of the phone. I have run out of ideas. There are no more trans-sexual haunts to tell him about, no more online groups that he hasn't tried. There are no trans women calling in, looking for a man to indulge their "soft, nasally voice" fetish. He will simply have to keep his eyes open as he goes about his life, like everyone else does who's looking for that perfect some-one who matches his or her fantasy.

Hopefully, he will meet the woman of his dreams some-day. I try to give him some encouragement before we hang up. I try to be kind – both for his sake and for my own, because I know that this will not be the last "looking for a transsexual" call that I will take. Maybe the next one will be someone with a fetish for slightly balding, big-hipped men with small feet. In that case, I *do* happen to know exactly where to find one.

Organ Trans-plant

WHEN I GOT my first PAP test and pelvic exam under a new insurance carrier, I knew there would be problems – and I was not disappointed. My claim was denied. As a man, I was not covered for that particular service. But as a financially struggling man, I was not going to just give up and pay the bill, either. And I knew that I needed to get things straightened out early on, in case any serious trouble materialized later. So I wrote an appeal letter to my insurance company that said:

> I am writing to request a review of the claim for myself, Matthew Kailey. I believe this claim was denied because it was for a PAP test and the insurance has me listed as male, meaning such tests would not be covered. However, I have female reproductive organs, which means that I need regular gynecological care and testing in order to maintain the health of these organs and of myself.
>
> I will continue to require ongoing gynecological care, and I believe that this service is covered for patients with female organs. Because I will require similar care in the future, I need to get my records changed or otherwise have this information on file, along with my request for a review of this current claim.
>
> The up side is that you will never have to provide treatment for prostate cancer.

Thank you very much for your consideration in this manner. Please let me know what other information I need to provide to you.

I was hoping that they had a sense of humor. Apparently someone did, or at least someone realized that the treatment I had received was appropriate. The denial was reversed and the claim was paid. Another "small victory." Another point for our side.

When I told a friend about it, he decided to take a chance with his own insurance company, which had already denied his claim for the same services. He wrote them a similar letter, and they reversed their denial and paid the charges.

This is not something that I do for fun, although I try to make it as pleasant as possible for everyone involved. These are the incremental steps that it takes to make inroads, to gain acceptance, and to change minds. Now there are at least two insurance companies – my friend's and mine – that are open to the idea that there is a diverse array of bodies out there.

Maybe someday, insurance companies won't set up gender-specific guidelines for health care. Maybe they will recognize that various people need various kinds of treatment and services, and that sometimes men need pelvic exams and sometimes women need prostate exams.

I know that some people won't like the fact that I refer to my organs as "female." The argument here is that, if they are in a man's body, they are male organs. I understand the argument, but my counterargument is that change takes time. Baby steps. And it's important when working with people to start where *they* are, not where *you* are, on any given continuum of understanding. My ultimate goal was not to teach someone to transcend the concepts of our gendered language. It was payment of a claim. I succeeded at that – and maybe more.

Plus it doesn't particularly bother me to see my organs as female. The longer I have lived as a transsexual person, the more comfortable I have become with being a "blend." It does not necessarily make it easier for me to confront the world – but it makes it easier for me to confront myself. And that's what ultimately matters – that, and not shelling out a bunch of money when I don't have to. Whatever I can do toward either goal is worth it.

Tradition and Truth

Scenario: I am standing in the kitchen with a nouveau trans woman as she prepares to host a party. She has been taking estrogen for about a year. I watch as she tugs at the lid of a salsa jar. After a couple of tries, she hands the jar to me. "I just don't have the muscle anymore," she says, rather helplessly. "I need a man to do these things."

Scenario: I am sitting next to a trans woman at a formal dinner. The plunging neckline of her gown that highlights her very visible cleavage seems only inches away from the slit in her skirt that travels up almost to her hip. Her make-up is flawless, and her long, red hair has been carefully styled. She is beautiful, and I'm obviously not the only one who thinks so. Her husband does, too. She laughs breathily when she tells people, "Oh, I'm just a suburban housewife."

Scenario: I am sitting with a table of trans men at a trans-specific gathering. A trans woman approaches the table as if to join us, listens in for a second, and then says, "Oh, you're just talking guy talk. I'm going to find some of my girlfriends." With a wave of her hand, she is off to find some female-oriented conversation.

Scenario: I am in conversation with a non-trans woman. Her hair is short and spiky, her face makeup free. She is dressed in what would be considered a man's button-down shirt and khakis. She is a lesbian and a feminist, and she is furious with some of her trans women friends who are reflecting the very female stereotypes that she has spent much of her adult life trying to obliterate. "Aren't trans people supposed to be defying gender roles and stereotypes?" she asks me. "I'm working so hard to get rid of these things and some trans women are just reinforcing them!"

IN THE TRANS world, there are many truths. One truth is that trans people and our allies can challenge – and possibly change – the very concept of gender, simply by being alive, by being out, by working for those changes, and by refusing to settle for second-class status in a world where civil rights are doled out in abstract doses for ambiguous reasons. Another truth is that we are under no obligation to do so.

It would certainly benefit almost everyone concerned, including the non-trans, heterosexual, mainstream population, if gender rules were relaxed. But trans people, simply by virtue of our transness, are not required to be the harbinger of these changes, no matter how much it would behoove us to be.

Many trans people have waited all their lives for legitimization of their gender identity, which sometimes includes all the gender trappings with which our society decorates that role. Whatever the true self is that has been forced to lie in wait for twenty, forty, or even sixty years, does it not have a right to come out in its own form when the time has finally arrived?

Gender diversity is a concept that is long overdue in our strict and structured binary gender system. But why is gender diversity only acceptable when it involves a divergence from standardized gender norms? If a trans person chooses to adopt facets of the established binary gender system in his or her self-concept, presentation, or lifestyle, that person is often accused of joining with the oppressor – the paternalistic and unforgiving cultural gender binary – and not fulfilling the mission of the more progressive gender movement, which is to eliminate the binary, which in turn will allow freedom of gender expression for everyone. But will it?

If our goal is to eliminate the gender binary and all the gender requirements that go with it, if our goal is to free ourselves from the oppression of gender expectations and allow freedom of gender expression for everyone, then it seems that those same freedoms should apply to every form of gender expression – including what some might consider over-the-top femininity or masculinity.

If a trans woman prefers high heels, silk stockings, flouncy floral-print dresses, or even plunging necklines, should she be censored by her own community for reinforcing female gender stereotypes? Is she adopting the roles set down for women by the oppressor, or is she finally expressing the personal gender identity that has been denied her for so many years of her life? Or is she doing both? And if so, which one carries more weight?

If a trans man goes out and buys a Harley and a *Hustler* magazine, has he morphed into the oppressor, buying into the very system that kept his own gender expression under wraps for so long – or is he simply, finally, becoming himself?

It's true that many trans people go a little overboard at first, moving completely and utterly into the traditional gender roles and expressions that our culture has already mapped out for them, then gradually moving back toward the center as they find their own personal comfort zone. But for some, their own personal comfort zone happens to be right where they are – in that ultra-femme or ultra-macho space that we often forget about or choose to ignore when we champion "gender diversity."

Is freedom of gender expression for only a select group of people? Or does everyone qualify? What is an "acceptable" gender presentation? And who gets to decide? If we fight for gender diversity, if we struggle for the right to express our gender in whatever way we choose, to live in our bodies as we want them to be, and to present ourselves on the outside as we see ourselves on the inside, should that fight not include every possible permutation of gender expression? Who gets left behind?

Plunging necklines, spiked heels, and "housewives" aren't the problem. Hard-core machismo and soft-core porn aren't the problem. The oppression of women is the problem. And the oppression of women exists independently of these things. Immutable gender codes, and the roles and expectations that go with them, are the problem – and they all exist independently of these things.

For some people, these things are visible representations of the problem, but for others, they are a natural way to exist. To deny those who would live within the rules of the binary the right to do so is to deny them freedom of gender expression – the exact opposite of what the movement claims it is working toward.

So what can we do? We can raise the stakes. At the same time that we're working toward the elimination of the binary gender system, we can work toward equalizing the value of all the characteristics associated with sex and gender, so that no matter who displays them – and in what combination – they are seen as worthwhile qualities to have.

Some human beings enjoy wearing high heels and make-up, while others prefer to shave their heads but not their legs. Some human beings prefer to take care of children, while others prefer to spend their days in an office or on a construction site. Some human beings like to talk about shopping, cooking, and home decorating, while others like to talk about sports, cars, and business. Some like to talk about all of these things and more.

It could be argued that anything a woman does, from cooking a meal to driving a forklift, is feminine behavior because a woman is doing it, and anything a man does, from playing major league baseball to crocheting an afghan, is masculine behavior because a man is doing it. This is the true beauty of gender diversity, and accepting it and embracing it are the true paths toward gender equality.

Scenario: A person with long, blonde hair, wearing high heels and a red silk dress, is getting a manicure in a salon while talking to two muscular, tattooed people – one with visible breasts and one without – about a television show that was on the night before. Another person – one with chunky streaked hair, eyeliner, and a visible bulge at the crotch – sits in a nearby chair flipping through a fashion magazine. A person in a suit and tie comes in to schedule an appointment in the hope that something can be done with the little hair that remains on a shiny, balding head. They all look at each other and start talking about whether or not it's going to rain. There are no questions, expectations, or judgments. They are all simply who they are.

Now, here's the $64,000 question – which one opens the salsa?

Staying Safe in Marlboro Country

I HAVE FOUND that male salesclerks can be particularly snide, especially if you don't measure up to their view of what a man should be. I do know the rules of football, but I don't follow sports, and more times than I care to count, the male clerks who have attempted to make idle sports chit-chat with me have ended up looking as if they can't wait to get off work so they can beat me up. But once, I was unusually lucky – fate was looking out for me.

I was reading the Sunday paper, searching for Dear Abby, when a headline jumped out at me. Terrell Davis of the Broncos was injured. He would probably be out for the rest of the season. I knew who the Broncos were, of course – I do live in Denver, after all. And I knew who Terrell Davis was, even though I couldn't have said what position he played.

I wasn't interested enough to read the article and didn't think about it again for over twenty-four hours. I had no idea that it had registered in my memory at all. But I guess my subconscious knew – more than I did – what information might be significant for a man to have.

The next night, as I was on my way to a friend's house, I decided to stop for cigarettes. I hadn't paid much attention to the fact that I was passing through a rather bikerly enclave – I think I was at the intersection of Harley Davidson Drive and Hell's Angels Avenue – until I had already pulled into the convenience-store parking lot and gotten out of the car. I wasn't afraid. I just knew I didn't want to hang around for any length of time.

Inside, the clerk had the Monday night Broncos game on. He was big and burly enough that he could have been one of the linebackers who couldn't make it to the game because he had to work at the Quik Shop and couldn't get his schedule changed. I asked for the pack of cigarettes, and as he rung them up, he grunted (and I'm not kidding), "How 'bout them Broncos, huh?"

Now I could have done what I usually do, which is to wave my hand around like I'm swatting at a fly and say, "Oh, I don't really follow sports much," but that didn't happen. I didn't even consciously decide against it, as unwise as it would have been. What happened was that, somewhere in the depths of my brain, some little cluster of cells designed specifically to keep me alive was activated, and I heard myself say, "Yeah, but I hear Terrell Davis is out for the rest of the season."

And then I collected my cigarettes, trying not to appear awed by what had just come out of my mouth, as the clerk stuck his hands in his pockets and shook his head. "Yeah," he said, "I hear ya."

I remained stoic, gave a little nod, and said, "I guess we'll just have to see what happens."

And then I was outta there – still in one piece and not looking back. My car was the goal line, and I made it there without getting tackled. Touchdown!

Let's See What You've Got

"I'VE NEVER MET a *female-to-male* transsexual before."

Yes, of course. I get this all the time from gay men. But this particular gay man had just spent the last fifteen years living in San Francisco. If a gay man lives in San Francisco for fifteen years and has never met an FTM transsexual person, I can only assume that he spent those fifteen years:

A) incarcerated.
B) homebound.
C) in a hut on the far side of Alcatraz island.

Almost every major urban center in the United States is teeming with trans men. If we don't live there already, we often migrate there in search of a more welcoming community, better access to health care and other resources, and a larger trans population with which to connect. San Francisco, with its rainbow flags down Market Street and its "anything goes" Castro district, is particularly attractive, especially for gay trans men.

In reality, my fine gay friend from San Francisco, who apparently had to come to Denver, Colorado, to actually *meet* a trans man, has probably met many of them throughout his decade and a half in the City by the Bay – he just doesn't know it. Thanks to the incredible transformative powers of testosterone, trans men rarely have to come out publicly unless we choose to, and we are hardly ever read as trans, even if someone is looking extra hard.

This invisibility is great for someone who is trying to quietly assimilate into mainstream culture, but it can lead to a lot of misunderstandings, unpleasantness, and even downright nastiness if the guy is simply trying to get a date or a trick for the night. A non-trans gay man can quickly turn ugly when he picks up a guy and then finds out later that his cute trick doesn't have the expected "equipment," no matter how hot the guy is overall.

This particular predicament is cause for ongoing discussion in trans man space: when, exactly, *do* you come out to your potential partner or one-night-stand? I always advocate for a "the-sooner-the-better" approach, primarily for safety reasons. I have no desire to be in a strange apartment in a strange neighborhood with a strange (and maybe rather large and burly) guy who suddenly feels that I have "betrayed" him by not intimately discussing my physical configuration beforehand. It's true that I might get rejected and left standing at the bar with only my beer for company, but I'll take that chance a lot faster than I'll take a chance with my physical safety.

The guys who feel as if they don't need to go into a "tell-all" confession prior to a little play have a very good point, however – how many non-trans gay guys honestly share their stats before leaving a bar or a party with someone? I'm not talking about all those 9-inched hunks who only seem to exist on the pages of the personals. I'm talking about real guys who hook up in real circumstances. Unless you both strip down right where you are and show each other all the goods, there might be any number of things about your trick that will disappoint you, and vice versa. These things don't come with a written guarantee.

So while I'm all for safety (mostly mine), I also understand the desire for privacy and anonymity, along with a person's right to possess the body he has without explanations or disclaimers. We're out there. You've met us, whether you know it or not. And we're not trying to fool you. We're just being ourselves, looking for the same things that you are. So – let's see what you've got.

The World's Smallest Penis

ONE OF THE benefits of working at a gay newspaper is that you get to surf very unusual Web sites in search of stories about porn stars or celebrities, so I wasn't really surprised when I looked across the room and saw my coworker watching an online video that appeared to be a parade of naked trans men who had not had genital surgery.

Of course, this necessitated abandoning my own story and getting up to see what was going on. And as I got closer, I saw who these guys actually were – contestants in a Howard Stern contest for the world's smallest penis. Now, I could win this contest hands down, but none of these guys were trans men. They were all non-trans men with itsy, bitsy, teeny weenies.

Even though the tape had just started, I could see that the first guy was the obvious winner. I've seen outie belly buttons that were bigger. The man was heavy, and that didn't help, but the fact was that his penis was pretty much not there. There was his stomach – you couldn't miss that – and below it was a smooth, triangular patch of skin (he had obviously shaved to enhance his chances of winning, if nothing else) with a tiny, round opening (his foreskin?) and a little bump – that was it. That was his penis, nestled snuggly in its little home, peeping out at the world as if terrified of what it would find if it emerged. There were several men behind him, but even from a distance, what they had was at least visible to the naked eye. They didn't stand a chance.

I have no idea what they were offering for a prize for the

winner, but it must have been a whopper (no pun intended) in order for these men to submit to this global humiliation. After all, we're not in ancient Greece, where small, boyish penises were prized. A large, sturdy member is considered the mark of a man in the United States, but here was a group of men showing the world, or at least the World Wide Web, that their mark was really no more than a dot.

And the strangest thing was that none of them seemed particularly concerned. Maybe they were just excited to get their 15 millimeters of fame. Maybe they desperately wanted that prize. Or maybe they just didn't care.

I made the decision long ago that I was not going to get any kind of genital surgery. There were several reasons for that decision – a lack of funds, a lack of the desire to go through the procedures that I heard some of my now-well-endowed friends describe, and, after a while, a lack of interest entirely. There came a point where I, like the guys in the World's Smallest Penis contest, just didn't care.

I would no doubt be disqualified if I entered that contest – the other contestants would probably complain that I had an unfair advantage. But any time that my particular body is considered an advantage, I'm in. Howard Stern, sign me up!

Short Fiction: Teenie Weenies, Inc.

WHEN I FIRST started transition, I also embarked on a writing career. "Teeny Weenies, Inc." was my first "real" published piece, appearing in the 2004 anthology *Best Transgender Erotica*, published by Circlet Press. I include a (slightly less erotic) version of it here, the only short story in this collection, because it reflects what I was feeling at the time about "measuring up," and my curiosity about how a non-trans gay man with below-average endowments might feel. At least I had an excuse.

꙰꙰꙰

HE MADE QUITE an entrance. No one had ever walked into a T.W., Inc. meeting with such confidence before. I had been attending the monthly support groups for almost a year and it had taken me six months before I could lift my head upon entering. Most new guys slowly shuffled in, examined the carpet, and then took a chair at the edge of the circle.

Sometimes the door would pop open a crack, then close abruptly, meaning whoever peeked in had changed his mind. It's not surprising. I have yet to meet a man who wants to admit that he is, at least by certain standards, microscopically endowed.

Maybe it's even tougher for a gay man. I could watch a night of porn or flip through any gay-oriented newspaper or magazine and come away feeling doomed. I had endured it for twenty miserable years before I found T.W., Inc., which stood for Tim Williams, Inc., the founding father of the support group that members had immediately dubbed Teeny Weenies.

I found Teeny Weenies on a website, a stroke of luck because I never would have called. Tim Williams, a 40-year-old gay man with a teeny weenie, was tired of all the pomp and circumstance surrounding big cock worship. He decided to found a group dedicated to the few, the not so proud, the invisible.

I had e-mailed Tim immediately, excited that I was not alone in Lilliput. He responded with an invitation to a meeting, which it took me two months to work up the courage to attend. Perhaps whatever cruel joke of nature caused our cocktail weenie proportions also caused us to be intimidated in all other areas of life. But not the new guy.

He bumped open the door and charged through as if he were a corporate CEO late for a stockholders' meeting. He made immediate eye contact with everyone in the circle as he looked for an empty seat. I have to admit that I was pleased when he chose the one next to mine. His confidence was attractive and the rest of him lived up to that initial promise.

He was short and slender, with small but well-defined muscles outlined by a fitted black T-shirt. As he strode across the room to his chosen chair, a shock of dark hair fell across his forehead and into his eyes. He sat and pushed the hair from his face, pausing to catch his breath.

Then he said, "Sorry I'm late. Couldn't find the place." His eyes swept the group as he smiled apologetically.

"Not a problem," Tim Williams said from the head of the circle. Tim appeared slightly amused himself at the newcomer's boldness. He had apparently grown used to the stealthy slinking of the new attendees. "If you'd like to introduce

yourself, you can. It's up to you. You don't have to say anything –"

"I'm Greg McIntyre." He leaned back in his chair and ex-
tended his legs, causing his pelvis to thrust forward and out.
None of us wondered what was in his pants. If he was here,
we knew – not much.

Several of the members murmured, "Welcome, Greg," or
"Nice to have you." I just gave him a sideways glance and the
hint of a smile, admiring the shadowy growth of beard along
his jawline. He winked. I yanked my eyes toward Tim, then
silently chastised myself. *He was flirting with you, you idiot,*
I thought, but the entrance, the full name given so directly,
the wink, were too much for me to handle. Sure, the guy was
good looking, but why was he so cocky when we all knew
he wasn't cocky at all? There were several attractive men in
the group, but they seemed to know their place. Good looks
don't necessarily go very far – usually only to the zipper of
your jeans.

Not that I would know. Small children didn't run screaming from me on the street, but I was far from handsome. This
was one of several discoveries I had made in my youth. At
fourteen, I discovered I was gay. At sixteen, I discovered that
cocks larger than four inches when hard were decidedly more
attractive. At twenty-one, I discovered that mine was not
going to grow anymore. And, throughout my adulthood, I discovered that I was "a nice guy," "sweet-looking," and "funny."

I would smile but cringe inwardly at these kiss-of-death
compliments that were always followed by the promise of a
phone call that never came. So I had spent the most recent
years of my life in the gym, developing a muscular body, which,
to my dismay, only served to make my cock look smaller.

My hair started thinning, too, just because it was *my*

hair. A glance in the mirror never failed to reflect a balding bodybuilder with a miniscule member, so I quit glancing. The mirrors in my house were getting as lonely as I was when I made my most important discovery – Tim Williams, Inc. And now I was sitting next to a brash, attractive man who seemed to have few qualms about his missing link.

"Would you like to say anything more, Greg?" Tim said. "You're not required to. You can tell us why you're here, if you want."

"I think I'll just listen tonight, if you don't mind. I'd like to get a feel for the group."

"No problem." Tim looked around the circle. "Anyone?"

"I'll talk," said Jerry, surprising no one. Jerry was a regular at the group and always had a pity-me story about his latest sexual failure. "I went to the bathhouse Saturday and met this great-looking guy. He was huge, too, hung like the proverbial horse. Well, he had rented a room and we went in. I still had my towel on, but he had been strutting around showing off his stuff all night. Man, I wanted him bad, really bad. Anyway, I took off my towel and he sort of looked at me. He didn't say anything and we actually had a pretty good time. But I gave him my number and he never called. It's Thursday now and he hasn't called. He won't call. He was polite about it and everything, I mean, he didn't say anything, but I know." Jerry shook his head and examined his hands. "I know."

"Wait a minute." My head jerked toward the sound in my ear. Apparently, Greg had changed his mind about just listening. "Are you saying he didn't call because of your cock? Come on, man, you don't know that. It could have been any number of reasons –"

"No," Jerry said. "It was that, I'm sure of it. He was huge, he was great looking, what would he want with me?"

"Superficial," Aaron piped up from the corner. "If he cares about the size of your cock, he's superficial."

"But you don't know that," Greg said. "You have no idea. If you think every rejection is because of your cock, you'll make yourself crazy. I mean, it was a bathhouse, after all. Not exactly the place to find undying love. And, anyway, speaking of being superficial …"

"Yeah," I chimed in, suddenly catching Greg's meaning and wanting to join up with him, impress him. "Who's superficial? All you mentioned were the guy's looks and the size of his dick."

"Right." Greg looked at me and nodded. "Exactly."

Greg didn't seem to notice the bemused stares that I was getting from some of the members. He couldn't know that I rarely talked and even more rarely confronted anyone. I surprised myself a little, too. Whatever he had going for him was tangible. I could pick it up and make it my own. It felt good, and I secretly plotted to save him a seat every time.

Jerry could not be dissuaded from the certainty of his inadequacy. Greg and I had formed a silent bond. I imagined a chill from some of the others for standing up to Jerry's whining, but, if it were there, Greg did not seem aware of it. As I played out scripts in my mind about asking Greg for his phone number afterward, the meeting continued on without me. Mark either had a new boyfriend who was a cop or he had been arrested and frisked. Sam had recently vacationed in Mexico and had sex on a beach or had read about it. I couldn't be certain and it didn't matter. The base of my brain was processing the threads of conversation, but my more cerebral self was scrambling for a plan.

When Tim announced the end of the meeting, panic set in. Greg stood up immediately and moved behind my chair as if to leave. I thought it was already too late when I felt his warm breath next to my ear.

"Let's get the hell outta here," he whispered.

I blushed with pleasure and anxiety, wondering if my thoughts had been so strong as to be obvious. He was halfway to the door before I was able to stand. I scampered after him, not wanting to delay so long that he changed his mind.

Once outside, he said, "Whoa. Some unhappy people in there."

"No kidding," I said, shaking my head in pity for the others as if I had stumbled into the meeting by mistake. "Oh, I'm Steve, by the way. Steve Abbott. You missed the introductions."

He shook my outstretched hand. "So I did. Okay, Steve Abbott. Nice to meet you. You know, I live just a few blocks from here. Want to come to my place? We could have coffee or a beer or something."

I agreed, trying not to get too excited. I had taken his side at the meeting. He was just being a nice guy. He probably had a boyfriend at home – one with a real man-sized cock. It soon became evident, though, that he lived alone. His apartment was a studio, plain but clean, with barely room for two of us as we bumped around digging for beer in the refrigerator. He didn't apologize or make excuses for the size. He just chuckled at our Keystone Kops routine and took my arm to propel me into the living room.

Once we had settled on the futon couch, which obviously doubled as a bed, I asked, "Why did you come to the meeting?"

He laughed. "Well, because I have a little dick." His smile was like the room, plain and clean. It enlarged the space while minimizing the distance between us.

"It doesn't seem to bother you."

The smile faded into an expression of agreeable amusement. "I can't let it bother me. You'd go nuts if you worried about stuff like that all the time. But I was interested. I wanted to see how other guys dealt with it."

"And?"

He adjusted himself on the couch so he was facing me and draped an arm across the back. His fingers were almost touching my shoulder. He still wore the half-smile. "Well, it's still different for me. Being trans and all."

"What?" I turned my body towards him, which caused me to back up slightly on the couch. I was instantly self-conscious because it appeared that I was backing away from him. I tried to casually readjust myself.

"I'm transsexual," he said, ignoring my clumsy wiggling. "You know, born a woman, didn't have no say, however that stupid song goes. I really don't have any dick to speak of. I mean, if you wanted to speak of it."

Now, I like to think I'm a man of the world, even though my world tends to consist of my familiar neighborhood, my boring job, and a lifetime of loneliness that I like to blame on my unfortunate genitalia. Greg was sitting next to me talking about his virtual nothingness, and the reason for it, as if he were mentioning that his car broke down. He was so smooth that, even with this revelation, I wanted nothing more than to impress him with my open-minded coolness.

In order to do that, I opened my mouth and squeaked out, "What do you have?"

He laughed again and took a long swig of beer. "If you're still here in an hour, maybe you'll see. Do you like chess?"

I nodded, although I had limited knowledge of the game.

This was evident when I was checkmated early in the first round. After he won the second round with ease, he got up to put the chessboard away, then sat down next to me, sliding his arm around my shoulders.

"You're still here, I see," he said. His fingers moved in small circles on my shoulder and across my back to my neck.

"I thought I should stay until I beat you at something," I said, then silently complimented myself on being rather witty.

"I'm sure we could find something you could win at."

His face moved closer to mine. I felt his breath against my cheek. He smelled of beer and patchouli and a hazy thickness that I couldn't identify. His other hand touched my knee and began the small circles there. I remembered trying to pat my head and rub my stomach at the same time when I was a child. I couldn't do it. Maybe he was equally inept at multiple hand movements. I didn't mind.

I was hard, and annoyed, as usual, that only the hint of a bulge showed at my zipper. Then I remembered that he had nothing there. Had he chosen me because he could not get someone more attractive, someone better looking, someone, well, bigger? He leaned closer and kissed me, teasing his tongue into my mouth until I could feel it against my teeth and gums, running along the edges then exploring more deeply, sliding against my lips as he pulled out. I looked at him as he slowly closed his mouth, and I realized that he could probably get anyone he wanted.

"Why me?" I asked.

"Because you understood what I was talking about."

His hand was at my shirt collar now. As the buttons came open, his fingers moved lightly across each section of chest that was revealed. No circles this time, but a soft back-and-forth motion that tickled and chilled me. When his fingertips feathered over my nipple, I looked again at my crotch, certain that the tiny bulge had grown to porn-star proportions, and was almost surprised to see that it was still barely visible. His hand moved to my stomach, tugging at the hair that grew up my abdomen and around my navel.

"You have way too many clothes on," he said to my belt buckle.

"So do you." I yanked at his T-shirt, embarrassed by my clumsy attempt, but he lifted his arms and wriggled out. Shirtless, he quickly slid his arm across his chest.

"What is it?" I said.

"Oh, nothing really. I didn't scar well here." When he moved his arm, I could see the thin white strips of scar that ran under his pecs. He pointed to an inch-long place near his underarm that bulged at little.

"You're kidding," I said. "After all this, that's what bothers you?"

"Hey," he said, with a mock-wounded look. "We all have our cross to bear."

"Let's forget about that." I was suddenly emboldened by the knowledge of his Achilles' heel. "You said I would get to see."

His smile returned. "And you shall. But to warn you – I haven't had surgery. Hormones produce miracles, but sometimes they're small miracles. Just call it enhancement of my natural charms."

He stood and undid his jeans. His body writhed slightly as he pushed his jeans and boxers as one down his hips and legs. Even in his thinness, his hips were wide, his thighs slightly fleshy. Voluptuous was the description that came to mind, and, although I had never associated that word with a man before, it became instantly desirable as my eyes roamed his body. A pleasant tangle of brown hair rested between his legs and, as if struggling to free itself from the dense thicket, a tiny dark pink head, like a cock for a Ken doll, pushed its way through. A warm sensation began in my chest and moved down to my groin. An uninvited smile broke out on my face.

"You're laughing at me," he said, but he was smiling, too.

"No. No, it's … amazing," I said, still grinning like an idiot. I wanted to bury my face there, to lick and suck on his tiny cock. I started to move towards him, still seated, at just the right level to indulge.

He backed up. "Uh uh," he said, putting out his hands. "If this is show and tell, then it's your turn. You still have way too many clothes on."

He again sat beside me, all skin and nakedness. Suddenly, my hands and mouth could not be controlled, and I lunged at him, sucking and biting on his shoulder and neck as my fingers roamed his chest.

"You're not making this easy," he said as he struggled with my belt.

I didn't want to let go of him, but I felt my cock straining against the confines of my jeans. It was my imagination, of course. My cock had never strained against anything in my life, but it didn't matter. I wanted out. I wanted him to see and touch what I had tried to keep hidden for so long. I got myself out of my jeans, and, finally freed from its denim prison, my four-inch cock sprung up straight and tall, as if pointing to something on the ceiling.

"Oh, man," he said, thrusting his face into my lap and taking it into his mouth as if it were the grandest thing he had ever seen. I started to think it was grand myself – so grand, in fact, that everything that followed happened too quickly. It was over too soon, and I wanted more.

He raised his head and swiped a forearm across his mouth. As he sat, his hand moved automatically into position over his scar.

"Stop that," I said, gesturing towards his chest.

He looked down, then dropped his arm. "Oh, sorry. Habit."

"Yeah, I'm familiar with those habits," I said, eyeing my rapidly deflating dick.

He kissed my shoulder, then moved his hand to rub the back of my neck.

"So," he said, "are we going to see each other before the next meeting?"

I closed my eyes and relaxed, enjoying the gentle massage. "Why do we have to go back to the meetings?"

"Umm ... because we have teeny weenies?"

"You don't need to go to those meetings," I said, opening my eyes to take in his body once again.

"Neither do you." He pulled his hand from my neck and rested his head on my shoulder.

"Hey," I said, "maybe we can start a new group – B.S.S., Inc."

"And that would be ..."

"Bad Surgical Scars."

I started to chuckle. He smacked my chest with his palm.

"Okay, smart ass," he said, standing. "If we're not going back to the meetings, you better just spend the night now. Get up. I have to make the bed."

I rose reluctantly and watched him pull on the futon until it enlarged into a reasonably sized bed, taking up most of the space in the miniature living room. As soon as the bottom sheet was on, he plopped down on his back and stretched out his naked body. The tiny pink cock had retreated into the depths of his hair and the folds of his skin.

I would see it again. With any luck, I would see it many times. He was drifting into sleep by the time I lay down next to him. Now all I had to do was wait.

Most Changed Since High School

AS I PULL off the highway onto Spencer's "main drag," I start to understand that time travel is, in fact, possible. There are the same pickup trucks, with gun racks and patriotic window decals. The same tidy homes sharing space with fast-food restaurants and corner liquor stores. The familiar sight of teenagers in the park, hunched over a joint of homegrown "Iowana." My small-town adolescence, thirty years behind me, is now back in my future again.

The Oasis Lounge isn't far – nothing's far in Spencer – and I arrive a little too early and a little too unsure. The pickup trucks parked at odd angles along the bar's fading stucco façade are merely updated models of the ones from my youth, driven to the local hotspot by a new generation of beer-drinking Iowa hunters and assorted other guys who just like the idea of guns. I let my car idle as I stare out through the windshield, trying to decide whether to park or drive away, waiting for someone – anyone I might recognize – to pull up, get out, and go in. Perhaps if I could join them as I enter the bar, what happens next might be easier. But no one shows.

If memory is correct, I had graduated with one of the most liberal, open-minded, and accepting classes that Spencer High School had ever produced. The Vietnam conflict was still grabbing the headlines, marijuana had found its way to Iowa and to the fields of our little farming town, and many of us believed that getting high and protesting the war were somehow related. We read *Rolling Stone* religiously. At parties, we tuned in to "Beaker Street," a late-night radio program out of Little Rock, Arkansas, that brought us the anti-war, rabble-rousing, drug-positive music that was censored by the top-40 AM stations we listened to in our cars. And we chose "All Things Must Pass" as our graduation theme, either for its ethereal, other-worldly connotations or as a tribute to the fact that the school would have to let us graduate, whether we deserved it or not.

But that was thirty years ago – as faded as the tie-dyed T-shirt balled up in the back of my closet. Where are those people now? Did they leave, like I did, migrating to Denver, Colorado, or some other large, progressive city and vowing never to return for more than an overnight stay? Are they living in urban hubs now, eating organic and voting Green? Or did they remain behind, letting the exhaust from the hot rods cruising up and down Grand Avenue seep into their being until they became one with this place, at first recognizing that there was no way out, and then, finally, not wanting to take that out, even if it were offered? If they actually did make it out, will they bother coming back for this one night? And if they stayed on, who will they be? And, most of all, what will they think of me?

Then, as my eyes scan the pickup trucks once more, it occurs to me that I have the whole night to decide whether or not I even want to be a part of this event at the Oasis – my thirty-year high school reunion. I don't have to decide in the parking lot. I can go in, sit at the bar, have a beer, and watch as my classmates struggle with each other's names or pretend to be friends with people they either loathed in high school or can't remember at all. They might glance my way, but they won't know who I am. Tonight, I can choose to be anonymous.

I don't look at all like the adolescent girl who walked across the stage to receive her diploma with long brown hair drifting down from her mortarboard and pooling around her shoulders. I look nothing like the young woman at the ten-year reunion with tight jeans and perfect makeup, and I bear scant resemblance to the semi-youthful woman in the miniskirt and high heels who had appeared at the twenty-year reunion with a bad perm and a burgundy dye job. I'm middle-aged now, but it's more than that. I'm unrecognizable to anyone who knew me when – even to my best friends. Even to the men who had hunched over me, sweating and panting, in the cramped back seat of a souped-up Chevy or a falling-down Ford. I'm a man now, a transsexual man, and until I introduce myself to my former classmates, I can remain an unknown entity – almost invisible.

I have no idea how the reunion committee reacted to the questionnaire I returned to them along with my RSVP. Maybe they were shocked. Maybe they laughed. Or maybe they just tossed it on the pile with the others. They didn't send my dinner money back, and I took this as a good sign – a sign that I would at least be tolerated, that I wouldn't be turned away. Remembering this finally gives me the courage I need to get out of the car, walk up to the door, and pull the handle.

There might be country music playing, or maybe it's pop. By the time I open the door and am assaulted by the sounds of a cramped and crowded small-town bar, I'm again numb with nerves and wet with sweat and wondering why I thought that even anonymity would be easy. A few people at the bar turn to look as the early evening light peeks in the opened door, but then they turn away again, back to their beers or their conversation, as if I'm actually uninteresting. Nobody gives me a second glance.

And why should they? These are the townies, the guys who drive the gun-racked pickup trucks, and I look almost like them – cropped hair, slightly paunchy, a mustache and a five o'clock shadow. For all they know, I'm one of them, some new guy in town stopping in for a drink after work. I could play out the role – sit down, order a beer, light a cigarette, and strike up a conversation. But I know nothing about guns, and I know even less about how to fit in with a group of hard-drinking, hard-driving, northwest Iowa men who have been men – and Iowans – all their lives, and who might not take too kindly to "my kind" in their midst, if word got around. And in a bar like the Oasis, word tends to get around. So I get my beer and head for the elevated dance floor on the other side of the room, where the women of the reunion planning committee stand in a huddle under a banner that says, "Welcome, Class of 1972."

The committee members see me coming. They all turn to look as I wind my way through the empty tables, my hands shaking, the steady thumping of a metronome in my chest. It's still early and I'm one of the first to arrive. I don't recognize any of the women by face alone. We weren't friends in high school. And they can't possibly recognize me, but maybe they've already put the pieces together – an unfamiliar man approaching the group as if he belongs there, but alone, not paired with a spouse from their class. Then, in an instant, we're all face to face – my face, unknown, right there – and I realize that I have no idea what I'm going to say.

But they're waiting. I've made the first move and now I have to follow it through – that is one expectation of a man. So I put out my hand, open my mouth, and what comes out is "Hi, I'm Matt. I used to be Jennifer Kailey."

And then I'm standing there with my introduction and

my hand stretched out awkwardly and my own private terror. Because these are the ones who have stayed. These are
women who have set up lives in a town that rarely makes the
map. These are women whose roots go deep into the northwest Iowa soil, who found husbands and jobs and a purpose
to carry them forward without ever having to go anywhere
else. These are women with small-town lives and small-town
values, just like the row of men at the bar. Maybe they have
warned their children about people like me – if they have
even been aware of "people like me" before now. Maybe it's
they who belong to the pickup trucks outside. And maybe
they won't want to touch the hand of a "person like me."

And then: "Matt, I'm Dorie Orris. Remember me? We're
so glad you came."

Dorie Orris steps forward from the group and takes my
hand in both of hers. She is round, like her name, and her
hands feel like a mother's hands, and her smile-plumped
cheeks shine pink through the dimness of the bar. I can picture her in a floury kitchen with her round, happy children
jostling around her, fighting over who will lick the batter from
the bowl. Her children are probably grown by now, but no
doubt they return home often to savor the hometown Iowa
cooking that they can't get anywhere else. I let her clasp my
hand for a moment, remembering that there really is such a
thing as small-town hospitality, and here it is – a live demonstration from a most unexpected source.

Then the woman next to her puts out a hand. "It's so good
to see you, Matt." I look at her and blink. She's familiar – petite and thin as a stalk of corn, with a graying pageboy and
black-framed glasses. I struggle for a name, and she sees that
and smiles. "Sherry Montrose. You look great."

There are five women in all, and each steps forward and

takes her turn. I can vaguely remember each of them – they were not the hoods or the homecoming queen, just regular classmates who have now made regular lives for themselves and who apparently have not warned their children about people like me. Because they are suddenly much more than I have given them credit for. They are more than just caricatures in aprons standing in farmhouse doorways and waving good-bye to their husbands at the beginning of hunting season. They aren't sitting on porch rocking chairs shucking corn or meeting at the Rexall Drug Store to trade town gossip. When had they all grown up and found a world inside of Spencer, Iowa, that I didn't know existed? When had they turned into real people?

Dorie Orris scuttles away and then returns with my nametag, which bears my high school yearbook photograph and says Jennifer Kailey in typeface, with Matt written underneath in black marker.

"You don't have to wear it if you don't want to," she says, the apology almost palpable in her tone. "We just ..." She shrugs. "We weren't exactly sure what to do."

"Of course I'll wear it," I say, and of course I do, pinning it on and feeling secure behind it, standing among the little group of women who are suddenly my brand-new friends. I figure that if none of us has to move, I can make it through the rest of the evening relatively unscathed.

Unfortunately, they do have to move. They are, after all, the organizing committee, and they have to greet those who arrive, even those who happen to be the same sex they were when they graduated. So the committee soon disperses, and I'm left at my perch on the dance floor to eye the newcomers, who at first trickle in and then keep coming, like the faithful called to a Virgin-Mary-shaped oil stain on the sidewalk. The music inches up in volume to swell over the humming noise of the crowd – the giggles and laughs, the shrieks of recognition, the greetings shouted across the room. I'm above it, looking down and wondering where in this crowd I belong.

And then I find out. It seems that, just by standing here alone, I have staked out male territory. Guy by guy, men begin to cluster where I am, alone or in pairs, removing themselves from the jumble below. I am the marker of masculine space, and the irony isn't lost on me, but I can't stand here forever hoping to blend in with "the guys." This is, after all, my class reunion, and I have just as much right to take a stab at nostalgia as anyone else in the room.

I finally see someone I recognize, both by face and name, and I attempt an introduction, although the noise is at full crescendo, and I have to yell to be heard. It worked with the women, so I put my hand out to Steve McDonald and say, "Hi, I'm Matt. I used to be Jennifer Kailey."

He shakes my hand and smiles, and for a moment, I feel as if I have discovered the magic words. It works. It works on anyone. And then he leans forward to examine my name badge and says, "Oh, yeah, Jennifer Kailey. Where is she?" And I realize that he thinks I'm her husband, come to stand among the men while she gallivants with her school chums below. Not so easy, then, with everyone.

"I'm her," I yell back.

"What?"

"I'm her."

Then Steve McDonald looks at me. Then Steve McDonald blinks. His smile sags, suddenly older than the rest of his middle-aged self, and he tries gamely to fix it at a point in time.

"Oh," he says. "Oh." And then the smile returns, too big, and he nods and backs up in a shuffle – not obvious, but almost as if he had lost his balance and was catching it again a few inches away. And before I have a chance to say anything more, he has conveniently found someone else to talk to.

I decide to soldier on, approaching the other men one by one for introductions. They seem to take the news well. They nod and smile and ask innocuous questions about my job or family life. But the questions are too bland, too everyday and matter-of-fact, and the ones unspoken hang in the air like the cigarette smoke that has started to fill the room, nearly transparent but obviously there.

Not all these men have stayed in town. In fact, many of them have gone on to the cities, to doctoring and lawyering and accounting, to rush-hour traffic, skyscrapers, and elevated freeways. But even big-city lives don't often include trans people, and it might seem ironic to them that they have had to come back to Spencer, Iowa, to actually meet one.

The women react even more positively to the news. The only one who seems aloof is Martina Finch, but then I can't be sure if she's offended by my present condition or if she still thinks, after all these years, that I wrote that nasty graffiti about her on the wall downtown by Feldman's Clothing Store. I didn't, but as cold and smirky as she is when I introduce myself, she can go to her grave thinking it if she wants to. Whatever it said, it was probably true.

And then, as I retreat from Martina Finch, I spot him. I don't know who he is, but I've spent enough time examining the men in the bar to know that he's the best-looking representative of his gender – our gender – in the room. I follow him with my eyes, trying to place him, but I can't think of anyone in our class who would have turned out this good – slender and well built, although obviously nearing fifty like the rest of us, with a thick cap of silver-gray hair that has decided to stay on his head and a matching mustache and goatee that highlight his streamlined face.

Who looks like this in Spencer, Iowa? In his black T-shirt and blue jeans, he could be a spouse, protesting being dragged to the event by throwing on the first thing he had come across. But it makes him look good, casually masculine. I don't recognize the woman he's with, and she looks much younger than the others, but she seems far more comfortable than he does, so perhaps she's just aged well. She's chattering and circulating, and he seems to be going along out of obligation.

I want to know who he is, but I don't know who to ask. My sexual orientation has yet to come up as a topic of discussion in the brief interactions I've had so far, and I'd prefer to keep it that way, since, at least in Spencer, I think things are best revealed in manageable doses.

I finally see that Sherry Montrose has taken a break from her duties as committee member, and she's standing on the dance floor alone, perhaps hoping for a few moments of invisibility. She doesn't get them. I sidle up to her casually and jerk my head toward the good-looking man.

"Who's that guy?" I ask, hoping that she takes my interest as mere curiosity.

She looks at me for a second, her eyes widening. Then she starts to laugh. "You're kidding," she says. "That's your old boyfriend."

"Oh," I say, nodding. "So it is."

But I have to examine him a few minutes more before I really see John Hickman, my two-year Spencer High steady, standing there in front of me with his silver hair and his sparkling wife. I have to look hard to see the jittery, testosterone-saturated high school kid who skidded around the Clay County fairgrounds on a secondhand motorcycle, with me clinging onto his waist, unable to ride on the street because he did not yet have a license. This isn't the boy who hovered over me every weekend in the back seat of a used Ford Fairlane parked under a midnight moon at the gravel pit. I know that he has stayed in Spencer, but he obviously no longer sacks groceries at Hy-Vee, and it's likely that he doesn't bus tables at Stubb's Ranch Kitchen anymore either.

Does he still help his parents park cars in their yard every year during the Clay County Fair? Does he miss eating Maid-Rites and waffle potatoes from a grease-soaked brown paper bag, like I do, or cruising Grand Avenue all night on a dollar's worth of gas, with his thirty-five-cent pack of cigarettes balanced on the dashboard and a can of Schlitz between his legs?

I want to know him now, but I'm uncertain what to do. It wouldn't be unexpected, given the circumstances, for him to reject me altogether, to turn away and tell his wife that he has no idea at all who I am or why I'm tapping him on the shoulder.

But I *am* tapping him on the shoulder. And when he turns toward me, I say, "Do you remember me? I used to be Jennifer."

And he nods calmly, with the slimmest of smiles, and says, "Yeah, I remember you."

He has not only come into his looks with a vengeance over the past thirty years – he has also perfected an incredible sense of cool. This is a grown man with a wife and kids and three decades of responsibilities under his slender belt. But I find out that he's able to maintain his cool because I'm no surprise to him.

"I saw someone from the reunion committee a while back," he says. "And they said, 'Guess what? Someone in our class changed sexes.' I said, 'Who is he?' and they said, 'It's not a he. It's your old girlfriend.'"

His smile is broader now. His wife, Carol, is one big bubble beside him, shiny and excited and filled to bursting with the idea of me.

"I think it's great," she says. "I've always wanted to meet you. And now, well, I just think it's great."

We spend forty-five minutes together on the patio, the three of us, and I receive an invitation from Carol to visit their home the next day – an invitation that I decide is best to decline. This is their life, not mine, and they need to be left to it. They shouldn't be forced to struggle with introductions to their children or explanations to their neighbors. They shouldn't have to rehash a past involving a person who, in some ways, no longer exists. And they shouldn't have to puzzle over the "what ifs" if things had gone differently.

John Hickman has done better than he ever would have with me. And I realize that I love them both now, in a way that is best left to brief and pleasant interactions on the patio of the Oasis, and that can only be damaged by attempting to make any more of this than what it actually is. It's not a friendship or a nostalgic bond formed around a failed and near-forgotten romance. It's the kindness of strangers, and I more than appreciate that kindness. This is, after all, still Spencer, Iowa. And John Hickman is still face-to-face with a man who used to be his girlfriend.

When we return to the dim light of the bar and the assault of the music, I yell into John's ear, "Where's the bathroom?" Without a blink or a pause, he directs me to the men's room, and I admire him even more.

But it seems that not everyone at the reunion has morphed into a grown-up Fonzie. The restroom, like the hundreds of public men's rooms I have been in before, has one urinal and one stall. The stall has no door. And the moment I sit down, the bathroom door opens. Then it closes again. But no one has entered. I hear muffled yelling and laughter on the other side of the door and realize that whoever had opened it has been sent in as a spy. We are all back in high school now, and there appears to be a burning question to be answered in the bar – am I standing or sitting?

And I understand that, although we've all grown up, maybe there's still a little something left over – something that causes us to snicker when someone farts or makes us want to throw a French fry across the room to get our friend's attention. Something that makes us squirm and pass notes during a boring office meeting or confiscate the pot from the children's bedroom and smoke it ourselves. Maybe a high school reunion is just the place to raise the ghosts of the people we once were, and maybe they just want to find out if there's a little bit of Jennifer left over somewhere.

Now they know. No matter who we've become, there are parts of us that will never go away – mine just happen to be a little more private than most. At least tonight.

I've been a transsexual man for several years and am used to the curiosity, the disgust, and even the hatred that I evoke in other people, just by being me. I speak about it, I write about it, and yes, there are even times when I discuss the "non-traditional" male body in which I live, the transsexual body that will always be mine and that will always force me to sit, rather than stand, in the men's bathroom. There's no shame in that, and most of the time, there's a measure of pride in knowing that I've finally become who I was meant to be, just like my classmates who are satisfied and comfortable with the lives they've made for themselves.

The world in which I now spend my time is one where it's not unusual for men to sit and women to stand, for men to put their feet in stirrups and women to turn their heads and cough, and where no one defines gender by the few square inches between a person's legs. The Oasis Lounge is not in that world – but I still am. And sometimes I think that the reason I exist at all is to teach others about my life, and the lives of all transsexual people, and to bring that world to places where it doesn't yet exist – like right here, in the Oasis Lounge in northwest Iowa.

This is as good a time as any to start, so I hold my head level and walk back out into the onslaught of voices, the blur of faces in a fog of cigarette smoke, the smacking of pool balls against one another, the music that is now just a garbled screech from the aging overhead speakers, and I show them the confidence, the courage, and the comfort of the world that I brought along to share with them. I show them the pride of a life well lived, however it is lived. And I show them – despite the minor inconveniences of living in a transsexual body, always hoping for a door on a public bathroom stall – what it means to be whole.

Acknowledgements

Thank you so very much to:

My parents, who were brilliant and fantastic, and who made me a better person than I could have ever hoped to be.

My blog readers (at tranifesto.com), who are also brilliant and fantastic, and who contribute their wisdom and insight on a regular basis. A blog is only as good as its readers.

My best friends Sean Gardner and Drew Wilson (milehighgayguy.com), who have gotten me through some rough times and some good times, and who have both been an endless source of support.

Anyone who is reading this book.

CPSIA information can be obtained
at www.ICGtesting.com
Printed in the USA
LVHW041713040622
720519LV00005B/313